HOW TO BUILD A BRAND
WORTH TALKING ABOUT

by Graham Brown
Jamal Benmiloud
Paul O'Shannessey

81% of people choose brands based on what their friends (not agencies) said

source - mobileYouth research

TABLE OF CONTENTS

BUILD A BRAND WORTH TALKING ABOUT

If customers like you, be afraid; be very afraid. Today, people only recommend brands they love.

If 81% of people choose brands based on recommendations from friends and family, why are CMOs still spending $130 billion a year building awareness and only getting "likes"? The reason is they are stuck with an ad agency designed for the last century.

Starbucks, LEGO and Apple built their multi-billion dollar businesses spending much less on advertising than their competition. Everybody's talking about these brands and their sales results speak for themselves.

Think that's good? On our quest to find the most loved brands in the world, we found a whole treasure trove of success stories - from retailer Zappos, to Chinese smartphone manufacturer Xiaomi, to Monster Energy Drinks - who spent little or nothing on advertising.

They all did it by leaving behind the old model of awareness and likes, and embracing their own personal armies of influential fans who loved the brand.

We wrote this book to help CMOs build a marketing team of millions. Create a brand worth talking about. Why settle for 2nd best? Why settle for being liked when you can be loved?

WHY DOES BRAND LOVE MATTER NOW?

৶৶৶৶৶

"In this ever-changing society, the most powerful and enduring brands are built from the heart. They are real and sustainable. Their foundations are stronger because they are built with the strength of the human spirit, not an ad campaign. The companies that are lasting are those that are authentic."

- Howard Schultz, CEO Starbucks

"It amazes me when I see brands so focused on how many Likes they can accumulate, that they neglect being "true" to their consumer. The ones I see standing the test of time remain honest and authentic to their original DNA. They never waiver from it, and their "audience" sees this and remains loyal."

- Mark Sperling: Red Bull, Troy Lee Designs, Live Nation, Tony Hawk

"Likes are the journey not the destination - building an audience of Brand Fans is just the beginning. It's the foundation of social media not the roof."

- Ian Stewart: Converse, MTV, Coca-Cola

"Liking a brand is a linear, rational connection with the content of a brand or company. Loving a brand is a nonlinear, emotional connection with the context of a brand or organization. Like is about marketing with consumers and followers. Love is about branding with fans and leaders. Liking a brand is non-committal and based on appointed authority and paid media. Loving a brand is a commitment based on earned power and viral media."

- John Waraniak: SEMA, GMC, No Fear

"Consumers today want to be loved, not liked. Brands can do this by weaving their products and services into the fabric of their consumers' ever-changing lifestyles and helping them to improve the quality of their lives and that of their friends and family. Once this mutual love affair happens, it has the potential to turn into a long-term relationship that is hard to break, and even tougher for competitors to swoop in and steal consumers hearts and minds."

- Vipe Desai: Monster Energy Drinks, Surfrider Foundation

"A *like* is a click, it is a vanity metric and a superficial measure of engagement. Love reflects consideration, depth of feeling and meaningful engagement. Not always easy to measure but you should know when you feel the love (and when you don't)."

- Vijay Solanki: Philips, Lastminute.com, Shazam

"The concept of like can be fleeting, a passing trend or fad. Love is for brands who go for the long term, created by how you act, embodying your promise and doing that consistently. The real question is once you have brand love, can you keep it?"

- Adam Boita: Pernod Ricard, Sony Computer Entertainment

"What brands need to focus on is spreading the love. A real deep-rooted love that cuts through the meaningless and sanitized brand 'moments' that clog up the digital and analogue airwaves. Most brands are caught up chasing fickle 'likes' that are ten-a-penny. What really matters are creating interactions and moments and mind bombs that really mean something to somewhere about their lives. Stuff that we watch listen read and then think 'Yup - been there, felt like that.' This is when the connection is made and the bond between consumer and brand begins to form. This is when the love begins to glow."

- Adam "King Adz Stone": Author "Street Knowledge" & "The Stuff You Can't Bottle"

THE TIN MAN'S QUEST

Dorothy leads a band of merry adventurers along the Yellow Brick Road in search of the Emerald City. It's a familiar story as told in L Baum's classic, "The Wizard of Oz."

The Emerald City is the answer to their quest. It's here the Wizard grants them their wishes: Dorothy wants to return home to Kansas, the Lion wants his courage and the Scarecrow his brains.

Perhaps the most iconic and remembered character of this tale is, however, the Tin Man, who desires only a heart to make him human again.

In Baum's original book, the Wizard grants the Tin Man's wish. But, as they leave the Emerald City, the Tin Man discovers the heart to be fake, made of velvet and filled with sawdust. Crushed, the Tin Man wonders if he will be condemned to live without feeling and emotion forever.

In the story's pivotal scene, Dorothy reveals to the Tin Man he doesn't need the Wizard's heart. The Tin Man had a heart inside him all along, he was just looking for it in the wrong places.

The Wizard of Oz is one of the most iconic and popularized stories of all time. Despite its fairytale status, the story holds key truths about our own weaknesses. We desire the new and shiny, the lure of the faraway and the quick fix of the expert rather than looking inside ourselves for answers.

And the same is true of marketing today.

We are an industry of Tin Men.

For years we've been following the Yellow Brick Road in search of the magic that will transform our brand: brand makeovers, celebrity endorsements, Big Ideas and advertising awards. It's a relentless quest that leaves us, like the Tin Man, weary and unfulfilled.

This is a book about doing it differently. What if the Wizard of Oz and the Yellow Brick Road was nothing more than a seductive myth? What if you didn't need to rely on the Wizard's magic after all and could transform your brand with your own people, right here, right now?

And, what if the heart of your brand didn't lie in the Emerald City, but inside your company?

A WORD FROM THE TIN MEN

৯৬৯৬৯৬৯৬৯৬

ENTER JAMAL BENMILOUD

Hi, I'm Jamal from the UK. I learned my trade at Red Bull and Monster Energy, where I was the VP of marketing.

My team's mission was to turn consumers into fans through innovative, authentic and meaningful marketing. In 2013 I set up a brand innovation partnership called EARN where we move our clients' brands' from like to love. Why aim to be liked as a business, when you can be loved?

At Red Bull we aimed for brand love in everything we did to build a business with a strong brand and sales for the long term. That is the secret of their success. And it doesn't just work for Red

Bull. When I left to join Monster, our goal was to beat Red Bull at their own game. It was a hard fought battle but ultimately we won, outselling Red Bull in the US for the first time in 2010; a position Monster still holds today.

What made our achievement both harder and more satisfying at Monster is that we did it all without paid advertising. Our approach from the beginning was to earn brand love and to create a loyal army of fans, to the point that they would tattoo the Monster logo on their bodies. By aiming to build high engagement with fewer consumers, rather than aiming for everyone to just be aware of us, we built a marketing team of millions.

It's tough because you have to take more responsibility internally, rather than outsourcing everything to agencies, but the rewards go far beyond the financials: it can empower and transform your people and the whole work environment. I spend a lot of time talking to CMOs these days and I find whether they are banks or car manufacturers, the challenge is familiar: most organizations are wedded to the old awareness-based marketing model and legacy agencies, which makes change difficult. But, I have found starting with small investments at the heart of the brand can prove the effectiveness of EARN's approach, providing a stepping stone to greater things.

This isn't just about cool energy drinks brands. We helped Castrol oil become the most shared sponsor of the 2014 FIFA World Cup (source Unruly) - our Footkhana film grossed 1 million shares, and was the most shared film on planet Earth that opening week. It's not just about social media shares either; our approach works in generating hard sales. We collaborated with three of the biggest YouTube superstars to create Limited Edition SIMs and helped EE, the UK's largest mobile operator, acquire 25,000 new customers overnight. Total sum spent on paid media advertising for both results? $0.00.

We're not anti-advertising or paid media, we just believe these investments should come much later on the CMOs' list to drive share and sales. We recognize that delivering earned impressions are harder to achieve, especially when organic reach through popular social networks is in such fast decline. But why not build your own brand platform for your fans? That's what we did at Red Bull because when you are in full control of your ecosystem, no matter how large or small, it's easier to move consumers from like to love, from customer to ambassador. Red Bull global brand properties such as the Red Bull Air Race, Red Bull Music Academy or Red Bull Racing were far more efficient than traditional sponsorship or advertising. Just type in 'Red Bull' to Google and you'll see the vast earned media this approach produces. As the CEO Dietrich Mateschitz said, "In literal financial terms, our sports teams are not yet profitable, but in value terms, they are. The total editorial media value plus the media assets created around the teams are superior to pure advertising expenditures".

Of course not all marketers want to change. There will always be marketers that outsource their work to the same agency because "they'll never get fired for buying media or making a TV ad". As they say, you can take a horse to water but you can't make it drink. That's why we spend our time backing the right horses, the ones that are already thirsty. These are the brave ones that dare to dream big and experiment small.

Yes, it takes time and patience, but that's why I joined this project - to help you see the possibilities for your own company. Great brands like Red Bull and Monster weren't built in a day, but with the right approach to people, culture and metrics, anything is possible.

ENTER PAUL O'SHANNESSEY

Hi, I'm Paul from Auckland, New Zealand.

As we speak, I'm writing to you from a hotel overlooking the skyline of Hong Kong. I travel a lot around the Asian region working with startups, with a focus on building their marketing strategy.

While my background is in startups, I have also worked in high growth environments with corporates: I helped Yahoo and APN get a foothold in APAC with their ecommerce sites. My link into this project came when I was brought in as CEO of Telecom New Zealand's MVNO "Skinny" (MVNO: mobile virtual network operator) to build an offering for the youth market.

Challenger brands like Skinny succeed because they are forced to think creatively. Startups have limited funds; expensive advertising is not an option. They have the passion and energy to take on the world, the agility to take risks and the discipline to focus on what matters - customers. As Jamal already said, these qualities alone are the fundamentals of marketing in the 21st century. When companies become too comfortable, lazy or detached from their market, they lose their edge and fall back on low-risk, low-reward strategies like advertising. Advertising is a tax on boring brands.

My first decision at Skinny Mobile was to fire the ad agency. We then recruited staff that reflected our customers and created a culture that we wanted to stand for. We identified and engaged our influencers, making them (not the Skinny brand) famous. Everyone became a marketer, everyone was a touchpoint between the company and our customers. Our customers loved it, welcoming them into their tribes and subcultures. Skinny became the #1 socially devoted brand in New Zealand (Socialbakers Report). We paid $50,000 to help co-create skatepark events with our customers, the same events large mobile brands were paying 10 to 20 times just to sponsor. By the end of the year, we had only spent 1/3 of our marketing budget.

Love takes time, both with personal relationships and brand marketing. Many companies today, however, are forced to take short-term focused fixes, quick-wins in the quarter to appease shareholders. That makes them look outside for answers when the solution is inside their own organization. They end up spending more on advertising but achieve less than ever. Take a look at the 10 year sales growth of Budweiser, the biggest Super Bowl advertiser of all.

My work with clients these days focuses on changes in mindset, not media. Marketing is not a division; it's a mindset. Your company culture has more influence over your brand than any advertising campaign.

It's not easy, start small, you will make mistakes, take a long term view. Try, track and evolve. Reduce the number of meetings, reduce the approval process, empower people and do something now.

ENTER GRAHAM BROWN

I'm Graham, a business author currently living in Japan. I say "currently" because I describe myself as a "road tripping entrepreneur".

Back in 2012, we sold all our stuff and traveled the world. It's a feature of my life. I've traveled over a million air miles in the last decade. Why? Because I love culture, seeing the world, and collecting its stories. In particular, I love collecting stories about amazing brands like those featured in this book, stories about their customers and stories about what drives us to behave in the way we do.

I first met Jamal when he called me in to work with his team at Monster back in 2012. Jamal was the only one on the Monster marketing team who wasn't decked out in tattoos, ear plugs and in a baseball cap. But, I guess that's why we connected. He wasn't trying to be something he wasn't and that's an important lesson for marketers today. I'm on the wrong side of 40 but still write avidly about the youth market. Sometimes what a business needs isn't a skateboarding teen to tell them how to run their marketing, but someone who has empathy, someone who can build a bridge between both worlds.

As for Paul, well that's a different story. Rumor has it that one of his team at Skinny photocopied my Youth Marketing Handbook back in 2010 and dumped it on his desk. He read that stack of paper furiously over the weekend then returned to the office to declare a radical change to the operator's marketing strategy. I don't know how much that would have cost him in management consultancy fees, but he still owes me $5 for that copy. But what's $5 between friends?

Like all good relationships, in life and business, it's an investment. You give first, get later. Brands are slowly waking up to that fact, but it's not an easy sell. You are up against the traditional advertising agency that doesn't like your CEO spending only ⅓ of his budget for the year or bringing in someone like Jamal to tell their client they can do it all without Paid Media. And of course, you're up against your own people. That's why we wrote this book. It was my job to bring these guys together and create a book about Brand Love that you can use for your own sanity. You see, marketing is easy, very easy. The real sell in marketing today is convincing your own people that Brand Love is worth the investment. And that's what great marketers do: Tony Hsieh at Zappos, Rodney Sacks at Monster, Gary Kelly at Southwest Airlines, Steve Jobs and Ron Johnson at Apple, Nick Woodman at GoPro, Jorgen Knudstorp at Lego, Wing Lam at Wahoo's Fish Tacos and Howard Schultz at Starbucks. All of these visionaries created exceptional brands by focusing on building Brand Love, starting day one, inside their own organizations. This book is about how they did it. We wrote this book because these are the stories traditional ad agencies don't talk about; these stories are the ammunition marketers need to create change in their own organizations.

WITH A LITTLE HELP FROM OUR FRIENDS

Like any good quest, you never complete it alone. So it's here we have to acknowledge the merry band of adventurers that helped us with ideas and quotes along the way. Thanks for helping us complete the adventure of getting this book published: John Beasley, Vipe Desai, Ian Stewart, Adam "King Adz" Stone, John Waraniak, Allan Price, Vijay Solanki, Zinnia Harris, Anna Greene, Sue Gurner, Leila Ghazai, Nichola Spencer, Adam Boita, Mark Sperling, Juliette Hughes and Gareth Johns.

CHAPTER 1. WHAT IS BRAND LOVE?

త్తత్తత్తత్త

Jamal kept twisting our arms about having a model to win reader attention. We were expecting one of those Monster Energy Babes as gratuitous eye-candy to hook you in, but he was really talking about the type of model agencies use to look intelligent. We had been writing this book for 2 years without a model, so we looked around for inspiration.

THE BRAND LOVE MODEL™

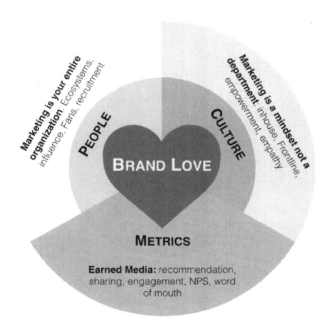

That model was right under our noses. Red Bull built its multi-billion dollar brand using a similar model. The more we studied it, the more we saw how it resonated with all the case studies in this book. Everyone talks about Red Bull and their content but if you go to the heart of their brand you'll find it's not about content but Brand Love. Red Bull's successful content strategy is the means to an end, not the end itself. Brand Love works. $4 billion in sales proves just how well it works.

So we adapted the model and made it our own: The Brand Love Model. We gave it context for all our case studies with the 3 elements of Brand Love: People, Culture and Metrics. You'll find that in each story, these 3 elements keep coming up. That's because it's these 3 internal features of marketing that define exceptional brands today.

A lot of clients ask us about Red Bull. "How did Red Bull do it?" and "How can we be more like Red Bull in our marketing?" In response, we'll pull out The Brand Love Model but with one caveat: why stop at Red Bull? If you think Red Bull is good, hold tight because we'll show you brands that are not only better than Red Bull, but also beat Red Bull at its own game.

JUST FOR FANS

Ok this is great, you're thinking, but we're not an energy drink, we're not cool, we're not based in California etc., etc... We hear you. Let's address those concerns first.

Yes, we confess, this book does have a strong West Coast bias. Hard not to have a bias these days when brands like Starbucks, Monster, South West, Wahoos, Uber, Apple, Facebook, Google etc. all operate from that hotbed of innovation. And while there is a bias that's reflected in how our media and technology world works, you're probably wondering if this model travels.

Is Brand Love relevant to fast growing markets like China where brands are still throwing billions at traditional advertising? Is Brand Love relevant to companies outside the action sports industry?

Too right it is.

Founder Lei Jun addresses fans at the
Xiaomi annual conference

Take a look at Xiaomi from China, the smartphone brand. Take this case study on board as a sign that while the case studies in this book are US centric (with the exception of LEGO from Denmark), the lessons learned can and do work anywhere.

Xiaomi is no global household name, but slowly and surely under the radar of mainstream media, it became the world's 3rd largest smartphone manufacturer in 2015 by valuation and 4th largest by sales. Perhaps the reason most people haven't heard of Xiaomi (yet) is that this Chinese brand won't be at the World Cup or paying for those expensive celebrity ambassadors that furnish your nightly TV screen.

When Lei Jun launched Xiaomi in 2009 with his MIUI operating system he didn't have any marketing budget at all. Rather than buy awareness, he set his team the task of building relationships at the Frontline of the developer community - its forums. When they weren't developing and bug fixing, Xiaomi engineers were interacting on the forums. In time, these activities became inseparable: early adopters of the OS not only provided invaluable feedback, they also got involved in the development process with their own ideas and patches.

Through the organic process of building Brand Love with fans, Xiaomi identified their top 100 power users to work alongside them in an iterative product development cycle. But it wasn't just the development side these Fans were useful for. They also became influential advocates of the brand. These "Me Fans" (as they were called) played a key role in curating content and conversations on the 1 million strong MIUI forum.

Xiaomi also worked with their Fans to organize offline meetups covering 31 cities in China every 2 weeks. Meetups gave engineers and Me Fans an opportunity to interact, an opportunity to join the dots. It's from this Beachhead of loyal Fans that Xiaomi's world domination plans began. Working closely together, Xiaomi developed and eventually launched its first smartphone in 2010.

The Brand Love model works. 42% of Me Fans bought MIUI smartphones. Not just one, but an average of 3! The MIUI 3 smartphone sold out in 2 minutes. Not even Apple can get close to that kind of Brand Love. But Xiaomi isn't resting. They're investing bigger than ever in their offline meetups, with between 300-400 offline held annually around China as well as introducing a new annual Me Fan festival.

Xiaomi goes from strength to strength. Will they become the first truly global Chinese brand to compete with the likes of Apple and Samsung?

It's a familiar story reflected in this book:

i.   Build a Beachhead of Fans that Love your product or idea. We're not talking about passive brand targets on steroids but customers who actively promote your brand and want a meaningful relationship with the company.

ii.   Join the dots. Build a community for your Fans, a platform for them to share and connect.

iii.   Work closely with your Fans to develop the product. Develop a rapid feedback cycle that allows product developers to implement Fan ideas quickly and without bureaucracy.

iv.   Launch product to wider market.

v.   Go global.

It's also the story of GoPro, Apple, LEGO, Monster Energy and so many other billion dollar global brands we write about in this book, and it works for startups in China as much as it will for brand turnarounds in Denmark.

The key takeaway from the Xiaomi story is that we have arrived in The Connection Economy. We have left The Ogilvy Era behind. Here is a brand that launched with no real mass-market product, with no marketing budget, in China. The fact that this company can now outsell rivals like Nokia and Microsoft with ad spends in the billions is testament to a shift in the marketing fitness landscape.

Xiaomi also proves Brand Love starts inside the business. Like their counterpart brands covered in this book, their initial weakness became a strength. It's precisely because they lacked a marketing budget when starting out that they were forced to think creatively. By thinking creatively, Lei Jun's team had to go direct to the customer and work. It could so easily have been different. Big ad budget, call in the agency pitch, wait for the results. Today, Xiaomi's forum has 10 million registered users who supply an average of 100,000 posts a day.

When you build a base of Fans this dedicated to your brand, your marketing dollars (and Yuan) go so much further. Compare Xiaomi's social media presence to that of rival big spenders like Nokia or LG:

TABLE: How Xiaomi is building out its brand (and winning) without traditional advertising

	Nokia	LG Mobile	Xiaomi
Date first phone launched	1987	2005	2010
Traditional ad spend 2014	$1.5 billion	$500 million (est)	$0.01 million (est)
Smartphones sold 2014	170 million	80 million	80 million
Sales growth YoY	-30%	+20%	+300%
Twitter/Weibo account	2 million	0.2 m (USA account)	2 million
Facebook/Qzone account	14 million	3 million	12 million

Xiaomi's motto is "Just for Fans."

It's a theme reflected in this book that encompasses two key messages we'd like you to think about:

i.   Brand Love starts with your own people - your employees and your Fans

ii.   Focus on your Fans - the details will work themselves out

But this book isn't about Xiaomi, it's about how any company can employ the Brand Love model used by brands like Xiaomi or Apple or LEGO to really kill it in their sector. To get there, to understand how to do it, we need to first look at *how not to do it*. How not to do it is also how we've been doing it for the last 50 years and it's now passed its expiry date. Understanding how not to do it could save your brand, your job and also a lot of heartache along the way. So, let's look at the cost of doing it wrong.

CHAPTER 2. NOKIA'S SEARCH FOR ITS HEART

ഔഔഔഔഔ

Nokia Brand Ambassador - Paris Hilton

LADY GAGA AND PARIS HILTON

A scantily clad Paris Hilton turns to Lady Gaga, thrusting a microphone under her nose.

"You are incredible, you are an icon," she fawns. "What is the inspiration for your music?"

Gaga mumbles something about the East Side of New York and David Bowie. It's difficult to hear above the growing impatience of a restless crowd. The crowd are here to see the launch of the Nokia 5800 but, instead, are made to sit through Hilton's giggles punctuated by the flash of paparazzi strobes.

"I read recently in an interview that you liked me and my sister," she says while holding a pout for the camera, Nokia held in view.

"I always thought that 'Stars Are Blind' was one of the greatest records ever," Gaga replies (referring to Hilton's own forgettable attempts at a singing career).

And so the interview continues...

It's a brand manager's wet dream: two of the world's hottest and most recognizable celebrities on stage endorsing your product. It's as many column inches, front page splashes and TV celebrity roundups as you can shake a stick at.

It's easy to see how all this publicity can give you a false sense of security.

That evening, brand managers and agency directors attended the Punk Club in London for the launch of the 5800. They schmoozed, tweeted and took selfies with Paris, Gaga and other celebrities.

After all, the Nokia 5800 was a celebrity phone. The 5800 was featured in "The Dark Knight" Batman movie a year earlier as well as in product placements for pop videos such as "Keeps Gettin' Better" by Christina Aguilera, "Womanizer" by Britney Spears, "Right Round" by Flo Rida, "Shut it Down" by Pitbull and "Waking Up Vegas" by Katy Perry.

For a brief moment, the Nokia 5800 story felt good. But, while media, celebrities and advertising agency people fawned, the customers didn't get it. In 2010, mobileYouth released a research note that read, "Hey Nokia - Remember Me?" detailing the unedited and direct feelings of teenagers who were deserting the brand en masse. To the question, "What do you think of Nokia?" one 13 year old answered, "Meh."

And here is the Tin Man's challenge. It's easy to become cocooned from the needs of a spotty teenage customer when you're surrounded by celebrities and agency account managers. Your agency is telling you how you are one of the most valuable brands in the world. Your marketing fills the pages of trade publications. You're winning awards. Peers and family post envious comments on your Facebook feed next to those launch party photos.

While brand managers and ad execs partied into the night, Nokia was slipping out of the public consciousness. To teens it was a joke, the same teens who catapulted Nokia into the limelight 10 years ago. Now, however, it failed to stand up against Samsung and Apple. So rapid was its decline that you have to wonder how something so successful could go so wrong.

Nokia's story is also the Tin Man's quest.

The Tin Man wants only one thing: love. We all want to create hordes of fans camping outside our retail store, YouTube homages to our product launches and the chatter of customer word of mouth. We want to win awards, not have to explain who our brand is to other people at industry events and feel the appreciation of our peers. That's why we turn to the Wizard of Oz. His promise is seductive.

Think of the Wizard's promise as less about delivering real love but more as a comfortable numbness. It's that same warm, fuzzy feeling climbers or sailors report just hours before slipping into hypothermia.

When a brand lives in the echo chamber of its celebrity status; when it becomes hardened to the everyday lives of customers; when brand managers look outside for answers, the brand slips into an inevitable yet comfortable decline.

THE EMPEROR'S NEW CLOTHES

20th Century Marketing Legend - David Ogilvy

If there's one thing we'd like to share with you in this book, it's this: the biggest threat to successful brands today is their own success.

Nokia was one of the biggest success stories at the turn of the millennium. From 2006 to 2008, Nokia ranked as the 5th most valuable brand in the world, according to agency Interbrand. Nokia sat at the top table with Coca-Cola, IBM, Microsoft and GE. It was unique in being the only non-American company in the top 5 and the only mobile phone brand in the top 20 (Samsung was number 21 at the time).

Forbes magazine ran a feature in November 2007 asking, "Nokia: One billion customers - can anyone catch the cell phone king?" The market was Nokia's for the taking. The only brand that could catch and destroy the cell phone king, was Nokia itself.

To understand why it threw its lead, we need to first retrace its steps, understand the trajectory and work out how we don't repeat its failings.

Nokia achieved global recognition through a highly effective marketing model. But, the mistake was that the model it built the business on stopped being effective in 2006. The model we're talking about is the marketing model of the 20th century: advertising, Big Ideas, brand stories, celebrities and visibility. It's a model shaped by ideas like:

- "positioning"
- "awareness" and
- "brand management"

It's also a model shaped by the writings of industry patriarchs like David Ogilvy. Ogilvy was a marketing genius. His ideas not only shaped advertising, but business in general in the 20th century.

Time magazine named him as the "most sought after wizard in today's advertising industry."

Others said of his publications:

- "required reading for anyone in business" (Media Week)
- "mandatory that everyone in advertising read Ogilvy's first book" (Business Insider).

The magic still lingers even in the 21st century: his old company, Ogilvy & Mather, recently scooped a prestigious Cannes Lion Grand Prix for its "Magic of Flying" campaign for British Airways.

Ogilvy's ideas cast a long shadow on the creative industry; that's why it's fitting to call his era "The Ogilvy Era". This is the era of Madison & Vine, Mad Men and TV ads from childhood you still remember today. So effective was the model of the Era that its ideas are still ingrained in everything we do today in the 21st century: how we recruit people into the industry, how we train them, how we measure them, how we think and talk about marketing, etc.

It seems almost unquestionable, heretical even, that someone like us should dare challenge the status quo.

That's why we wrote this book. Like the story of Hans Christian Andersen's "The Emperor's New Clothes", where the Emperor proudly parades naked in front of his coterie of advisers believing his new suit is invisible only to the incompetent, it takes the naïveté of a child to point out the obvious...

"Oi! Advertising... you don't have any clothes on!" If we weren't to dare, this book would never be written.

FROM THE OGILVY ERA TO
THE CONNECTION ECONOMY

In the Ogilvy Era, it was the creative agencies that did the heavy lifting. They created brand stories. They bought media space. They decided how your brand would play out in the public conscious. It was fitting, therefore, that creative agencies became the stars of the era. Creative directors achieved celebrity status among their peers, agencies picked up awards and client brand managers just signed off on the budget to make it all happen.

It was a simple model: hire the best creative agency in town, assign the biggest possible budget, sit back and wait for the results to happen

While this model served the industry so well for more than 50 years, it fell apart when the media landscape shifted. Between 2006 and 2008 we saw the rapid growth of social media. Facebook, MySpace and Twitter all launched in a space of 2 years. During this period, social media went from near-zero to hundreds of millions of people.

On the face of it, the Ogilvy Era was still working. Brands like Nokia were able to throw spectaculars like the 5800 launch; the award shows were glitzier than ever and who cares what teenagers think anyway? Beyond the veneer of normality lay a fundamental shift that was redefining how marketing would work in the 21st century.

In the Ogilvy Era, stories spread through official, centralized channels. You bought media space on a TV network because you were pretty sure a certain group of customers would be watching at a certain time. Today, however, it doesn't work like that.

Stories spread fast between customers.

If you discover a fantastic coffee in town, you take pictures on Instagram, tweet your experience and share it on Facebook. Not only does this experience spread to your immediate network but, through sharing, it spreads into their networks too.

Imagine how that changes how people experience brands. Previously, you found out about brands through the TV, on the radio or in a magazine. Today, you find out about the same thing through people sharing those experiences in your network (even when they're in the bathroom).

We trust the experiences of our networks far more than official media. A friend reviewing a cafe is far more trusted than a review in a magazine, even though the latter is written by a "professional" with years of experience.

This is the Connection Economy, where experience moves fast and wide.

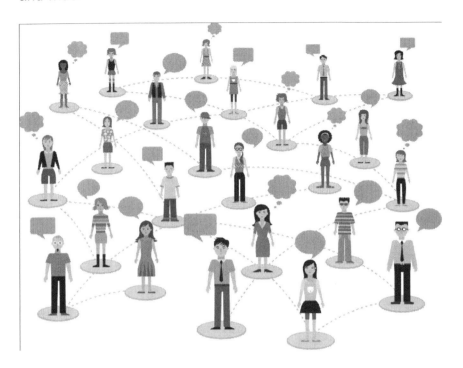

If you walk into a retail store and have a bad experience, you don't just tell your spouse over dinner, you now go and tell the world. If a call center rep delights you over the phone, the internet will be sharing that story for years to come.

What's changed isn't just how stories spread but also who's involved in the spreading of the story. In the Ogilvy Era, the storytellers were the creative agencies. They were the ones who crafted powerful brand narratives.

Today, in The Connection Economy, everyone becomes a marketer by default. We're not just talking about your customers. Think about how every single person in your business has become a marketer too. They all have their own networks, they all talk about your brand on a daily basis. Your marketing team, your call center staff, your HR people, your CEO and your retail Frontline - everyone is connected to everyone else.

When the CEO stands up on stage and tells the story of how the company began, she's a marketer. When the retail manager discusses with his store staff how they'll increase repeat business this quarter, he's a marketer. When the HR manager chooses a new field sales manager based on his personal network rather than qualifications or experience, she's a marketer.

When a call center rep creates a positive brand experience with every call, customers then talk about their experience to coworkers who then talk about it with husbands at dinner.

So, yes, to answer the Ogilvy Era diehards - people still watch and are aware of advertising, whether it's on TV or social media. But the key here is that the "official" brand story is just one of many stories out there today about your brand.

Just look at the data: 81% of customers under the age of 30 buy smartphones today because of what their friends said. Think about what that meant to Nokia. Before The Connection Economy, Nokia's official marketing could influence nearly 100% of phone purchase. Today, it counts for less than 20%.

Any brand committing the majority of its marketing budget to a strategy that yields the minority of its results is destined to failure.

BRAND IS EVERYDAY INTERACTION

Management consultancy PWC claims that 85% of brand is defined by everyday interaction. Everyday interaction means how customers interact with your retail staff, your call center and your own employees. That's where brand happens today. That means the whole direction of marketing is changing.

In the Ogilvy Era, brand started outside the company with agencies, celebrities and media owners. Today, in the Connection Economy, brand starts inside the company and works its way out. Because your employees, Fans and customers are all connected, the enthusiasm of your own people becomes the starting point for how others experience the brand on a daily basis.

This is the fundamental shift that caught Nokia out. Nokia was still playing by the old rules of building its brand **outside** the business. And it's not just Nokia; many brands are still stuck in the echo chamber of the Ogilvy Era because it feels good.

But not all. And this is what we want to share with you in this book. Many brands aren't stuck in the Ogilvy Era and it's category leaders that are blazing success trails for the rest of us to follow.

Apple, Starbucks, SouthWest Airlines, Zappos, Monster Energy Drinks, LEGO, Wahoo's Fish Tacos and GoPro. These are just some examples of brand case studies we'll talk about in this book, brands that made the switch. They don't look outside for their brand anymore; they start right here, right now inside their own businesses.

REDISCOVERING THE HEART OF
THE NOKIA BRAND

The Connection Economy brings with it a new paradigm in transparency. After all, 80% of people claim they updated their social media while sitting in the bathroom. Our point is that everything gets shared everywhere and all the time. This means that brands become less about the stories people craft for themselves and more about what the market decides that story is.

In the Connection Economy, your brand is based on a single truth. This is the heart of your brand. It's not what your creative agency says. It's what your Fans say.

As Clayton Christensen, author of The Innovator's Dilemma, said, *"Decide what you stand for and then stand for it all the time."*

Find that brand truth; stick with it for all time. Don't go looking outside for answers. Those days are over. Brand isn't defined on the outside by creative agencies. Brand isn't defined anymore by brand templates, websites, logos, campaigns, celebrities, ambassadors, sponsorships or awards. Brands aren't so much defined by your products either, but by the people behind those products because it's people, not products, who we share with and believe in.

With this brand truth in mind, could Nokia still be #1 in The Connection Economy?

Quite possibly, yes.

You see, Nokia had a strong brand truth before its celebrity facelift. There was a time when teenagers would look at pictures of snowboarders, see the blue and white logo, then ask, "Who is this Nokia?" Few knew Nokia hailed from the colder climes of Northern Europe but all knew it was something to do with the achingly cool emerging extreme sports scene, that it was rugged enough to withstand being buried in snow, a fall on hard ice or condensation on the screen from being buried in a warm parka pocket out on the piste. A whole generation grew up thinking Nokia was cool.

If you want to understand what lay at the heart of this brand love for Nokia, look no further than the word, "Sisu."

In Finnish, Sisu means determination, bravery, and resilience. Sisu is about taking action against the odds and displaying courage and resoluteness in the face of adversity. Sisu is a way of thinking that contains millions of stories and conversations. Sisu helped Finland defeat Russian invaders in the Second World War. Here was a makeshift army often equipped with only rudimentary supplies of wood and kerosene fighting the military might of a superpower equipped with T32 tanks, artillery and the latest machine guns. But Finns are hardy folk, scratching out a living above the Arctic Circle in those long, dark winters. They developed innovative forms of resistance, such as jamming logs in the caterpillar tracks of tanks. It was their Sisu that slowed and defeated the mighty Russians.

Sisu is a source of national Finnish pride. There was once a story in the Finnish papers where a fisherman dropped his Nokia phone into the water. Two weeks later it was found in the belly of a fish, still working!

Nokia built its brand on this legacy of consistency and reliability. When teens bought their first phone, it was a Nokia. When grandparents bought their first phone, it was a Nokia. 300 million people a year in Asia were buying their first phones. Back in 2008, the Nokia brand was more recognized than either Nike or Toyota because it wouldn't let them down.

Reliable doesn't mean boring. On YouTube you can find thousands of videos celebrating the Sisu spirit of the now discontinued Nokia 3310. This rather unimposing brick-like phone has little to shout about in comparison to its sleek, brash smartphone cousins but unlike these newcomers, the 3310 has Fans.

Youtube channel GizmoSlip wanted to see just how tough the old candybar Nokia 3310 really was. In their video experiment, the modern Lumia 900 failed a simple drop test, glass cracking on impact. The rugged 3310, however, with its simple LCD display and plastic case, was reasonably unscathed by the impact.

Running a simple drop-test was not enough. GizmoSlip wanted to know how these phones would perform under the impact of a 4 foot (1.2m) long sledge hammer, powerful enough to crack the bones of a man or smash a reinforced car windshield. Predictably, both phones were bashed to pieces. The Lumia lay lifeless; a battered, cracked hull barely distinguishable under a pile of crystal glass. The case of the Nokia 3310, although in pieces, could be easily put back together. Once reassembled, GizmoSlip pressed the "on" button and the 3310 was back in business!

Such is the prowess of the indestructible Nokia 3310. Many brands will spend a lifetime and fail at earning a moniker such as "The Terminator", "The Chuck Norris of phones", "indestructible" or even "reliable". On YouTube alone there are 66,000 videos about this "genetic throwback" celebrating its resilience and indestructible nature:

- Drop tests
- Will it blend?
- Why Nokia 3310 is better than the iPhone 6
- Nokia 3310 vs Armor Piercing 50 cal rounds

- Nokia 3310 crash test
- Nokia 3310 coca cola test
- Nokia 3310 pepsi test
- Nokia 3310: a brief history of the indestructible phone
- Axe vs Nokia 3310: how tough is tough?
- Microwaving my new Nokia 3310
- Nokia 3310 bat and wall impact

None of these videos are sponsored by, or produced by, Nokia. All these videos are created by customers, ex-customers and enthusiasts and they reflect the widely-held truth held by Fans about the Nokia brand.

The top rated comment on GizmoSlip's video is telling:

"This is fake because the hammer should break into a thousand pieces."

WHAT HAPPENS WHEN YOU DON'T LISTEN TO YOUR HEART

In the Ogilvy Era, Nokia's brand was what the agency said it was. When brands became tired, they charged agencies with a makeover, a relaunch or a refresh. A new "Big Idea" could transform a brand and its respective business.

Faced with the growing threat of Apple and its sleek designs, Nokia became ashamed of its Sisu heritage. Rather than build on what people knew and respected it for, Nokia's agencies started toying with the idea of "elegant design". They released lengthy in-depth videos detailing the philosophy behind the design.

To the surprise of its many Fans, these videos portrayed a brand that wasn't rugged or reliable anymore, but an Apple iPhone wannabe. Nokia was now from Pleno or Cupertino. It's as if Nokia was mortally embarrassed by the surprise visit of their hick country cousins from the banks of the Nokianvirta River in Finland where they originally came from. Nokia was more comfortable basking in the fake limelight of the photographer's strobes than in the simple, honest, workaday clothes of its founders. Nokia was now as believable as the kid who went to the big city and changed his name, accent and backstory.

Jeff Bezos, CEO of Amazon says that "*your brand is what other people say about you when you're not in the room.*"

It's an important quote for marketers in the Connection Economy for 2 reasons:

1) We are no longer in the room. Gone are the days when we were guaranteed a place in the conversation by virtue of TV sets everywhere broadcasting our message. Brand conversations are

happening everywhere and everyday. We have to accept we're not part of them anymore.

2) Your brand is what other people say about you. What customers experience and share about your brand everyday becomes your brand. It doesn't matter what you say your brand is. All that matters in The Connection Economy is what other people say and feel about your brand.

Even the Wizard of Oz admitted that, *"a heart is not judged by how much you love; but by how much you are loved by others."*

CHAPTER 3. DEMYSTIFYING THE BRAND

❧❧❧❧❧

In this book, we profile 10 brand case studies:

- Nokia
- Zappos
- Apple iPod
- LEGO
- Monster Energy Drinks
- Southwest Airlines
- Wahoo's Fish Tacos
- Apple Store
- Starbucks
- GoPro

We want to show you the winners and losers of The Connection Economy. We want to show how brand today isn't what it was 20 years ago, let alone 5. The rules have changed. Look at Nokia's decline if you want evidence that playing by the same rules is going to get you the same results.

We also want to demystify the whole marketing process. Brand isn't something mystical like the hocus-pocus of the Wizard from the Emerald City. Many agencies benefit from this mysticism because it reinforces client dependence. The more agencies try to obfuscate the brand process, the more they disempower client brands, the more they can charge.

David Ogilvy once wrote that brand was, "the intangible sum of a product's attributes: its name, packaging, and price, its history, its reputation, and the way it's advertised."

That's right, Ogilvy said brand was intangible: it cannot be touched or grasped; it has no physical presence; and by being intangible we can neither measure nor see it objectively.

David Ogilvy died in 1999. That wasn't just another century, but also another millennium.

It's time to say goodbye to The Ogilvy Era and the Yellow Brick Road distraction of industry chatter, agency pitches and their awards.

We can do that right now by bringing brand into the light and removing its mysticism and reverence. In sharing these 10 case studies we hope to prove that brand isn't the wizardry of an agency. Brand is simple, everyday mechanics. And because it's simple and everyday, any company can get it right today if they start inside (not outside) the business.

Throughout the case studies in this book you'll find that brand is the product of 3 fundamentals that start inside the business to earn Brand Love:

People, Culture and Metrics.

Go back to the Brand Love model. What the brands do *differently*; how these brands nurture Brand Love; rather than look outside for the answer, they focus inside the business; they focus on the 3 fundamentals.

These are the 3 key mechanics of brand we'll be focusing on in this book and we've laid them out in this table to show how they've changed:

	OLD	NEW
Time	The Ogilvy Era (20th Century)	The Connection Economy (21st Century)
People	Experience, managers, celebrities, brand ambassadors, recruitment HR function, agency selection	Ecosystem, Influence, Fans, entire organization, recruitment is marketing, peer to peer, Collaborators/co-creators
Culture	Efficiency: Outsource, Empowering Agency, Marketing is a department	Empathy: Inhouse, Empowering Staff, Marketing is a mindset
Metrics	Awareness, top of brand, recall, brand equity	Recommendation, content shares, word of mouth, engagement, NPS*

METRICS: We have to use metrics that encourage our conversations to last. We want people to stay and talk. We want people to see relationships as key to growth, not as obstacles to next month's KPI.

CULTURE: We have to create cultures that encourage our people to interact and cultures that encourage Fans to interact with one another. We need to lead by example and show that each and every one of us needs to get out there and create a positive brand experience.

PEOPLE: We need people who get it. We need people who love interacting. We need to recruit people who share the same passions as the Fans and empathize with their needs rather than people who want to manage and control markets.

NPS: Net Promoter Score is measured by asking customers "on a scale of 1-10 how likely are you to recommend this brand to a friend?" So, a high NPS score means people talk about the brand.

CHAPTER 4. THE HEART OF THE ZAPPOS BRAND

❧❧❧❧❧

Zappos CEO - Tony Hsieh

THE ZAPPOS BRAND IN ACTION

"Whoever is in charge knows what they are doing!

I have returned items to other retailers in the past ... to experience a wait of 15-45 days to see my refund hit my account, typically with the return shipping cost deducted. Most return policies are within 30 days from 'order' ... not receipt.

Zappos is 365 days from receipt.

And ... the final touch of class, a timely, common sense e-mail notification that my refund is in process including helpful information that may affect the process. I am also a fan of the online video excerpts of 'all' products. VERY SMART for any online retailer ... but very few provide ... and I think Zappos was the first. And, I love Option #5 on your Customer Service Phone Line.

You are not intrusive like most online retailers ... bombarding me with a constant barrage of emails. Delete, delete, delete. And now ... Brand X = Annoying. When I see an email from Zappos ... I know it is worth my time to read. I have not had that much direct contact with your employees...because your online system is so user friendly. But, it feels like I have with every transaction I have had with you.

When I think of Zappos.....I see smiling, helpful faces.

How did you do that?"

- Jill K from Stuart, Florida

(Customer feedback on Zappos website.)

When it comes to brand, Zappos knows what it's doing.

Zappos rarely advertises or employs the services of a creative agency. It doesn't run a customer loyalty program, offer heavy discounts or hire celebrities. Take a look at the numbers: 75% of business comes from repeat customers. That kind of brand loyalty is not only world class, it's virtually unheard of. No wonder Amazon bought Zappos for a billion dollars.

To understand what makes the Zappos brand a success, we need to lift the lid on the company and understand how they operate. After all, this is an online shoe retailer. What's so special about that? There are a hundred such retailers at the end of a Google search. Zappos doesn't even sell its own shoes, rather shoes that any other retailer could sell with the right relationships.

So, just how does Zappos do it?

To answer Jill K's original question, we need look no further than a prominent wall in Zappos' Las Vegas HQ. The wall is decorated with neckties cut in half, underneath which the names of staff members.

At the bottom of the wall, a sign reads "no ties allowed". There is your answer. Zappos is different and it's this difference that makes the brand exceptional.

Let's have a look at some of the evidence:

- Zappos responds to 100% of customer service inquiries within 24 hours (according to research from StellaService)
- Zappos practices what it calls "Holacracy", a flat organizational structure with minimum hierarchy
- Zappos' call center staff don't use scripts

Already we can see that this is no ordinary retailer. It's a little quirky and takes a few risks. But the key to replicating its success lies in understanding that Zappos is no gimmick. Success in the Connection Economy is not about social media, ping pong tables and funky offices with slides, but what lies at the heart of the brand.

BUILDING THE BRAND FROM THE INSIDE OUT

Zappos builds its brand inside the business. As Dorothy said, "look inside to find your heart". Everything comes from word of mouth and that starts inside the business with its own employees.

It takes discipline to focus on the heart of the brand. At the heart of Zappos, and every successful brand in this book, are 3 fundamentals: People, Culture and Metrics. Think of these as your brand DNA. They are the truth about your brand that, over the long term, will always bear out. No matter how much you spend on advertising, social media or product launches, your brand will always gravitate back towards the experience created by your People, Culture and Metrics.

Let's examine them a little more in depth here:

PEOPLE: what people (employees & customers) say about your company.

CULTURE: how you treat and recruit these people.

MTERICS: how you measure and reward them.

This is the heart of your brand. Get these 3 fundamentals right and everything else - from your choice of marketing agency to your logo - falls into place.

That's the challenge. The "everything else" is the easy part. It's easy to assign a budget to a marketing agency. It's easy to plan a product launch or sit through a pitch from a brand makeover. Sure, it's hard work, but when we mean "easy" we mean you're not challenged to think differently or take risks; you just follow the Yellow Brick Road.

You have to say "no" to the distractions. You have to keep focused on the action that requires more work. You have to be comfortable with asking the uncomfortable questions.

PEOPLE: BRAND STARTS WITH RECRUITMENT

Traditionally, the "people" aspect of business was an HR concern. Recruitment, employee morale and remuneration all happened in a different department to the one that looked after marketing. But, Zappos challenges this approach, starting day 1 with recruitment.

Like most companies, Zappos places importance on the recruitment process, nothing new there. The difference is the "moment of truth" where the company and candidate assess their mutual fit. In the traditional model, it would be the HR and recruiting manager who'd arrive at a decision. Zappos, though, is different.

4 weeks into the recruitment process, Zappos candidates receive what is known as "The Offer." The Offer states, "quit today and we'll give you $4,000 in cash. Stay and we'll offer you employment at Zappos." Quit and get paid $4,000 or stay and get employment? For many, The Offer seems counter-intuitive and open to abuse. That would encourage carpet-baggers only interested in the 4 grand payoff.

If you invest in your people, they will build a strong business for you.

Let's think this through a minute, starting with counter-intuitive. Some companies today offer signing-on bonuses as a way of securing talent. Critics would argue that Zappos, by contrast, is rewarding failures when they should be using the money to attract talent.

But, it doesn't work like that. Go back to the statistics. 75% of Zappos business is repeat customers. Unlike competitors, Zappos wins out because it's focused on the long term and to nurture that kind of outlook you need people who also think long term. Short term focused people grab chances whenever they see them and $4,000 is tempting. It takes a special kind of person to forego $4,000 because they see greater rewards working long term with your company.

But what about attracting carpet-baggers? How does Zappos weed out those who game the system? The Offer also commits management to the recruitment process. Nobody wants to be the manager that pays $4,000 out of their budget to someone gaming the recruitment process. People hoping to game the system, short-term thinkers and those who just don't fit are weeded out early on. Managers make sure that they're recruiting the right people from day 1. The recruitment process is tough (as we'll discover later on) and it involves many aspects that aren't considered in traditional brands e.g. asking the company taxi driver how the candidate greeted and thanked them before and after the interview. Like the brand, you can't fake this stuff. Experience spreads, starting with the truth about who you are and how you interact with others.

You may or may not be able to introduce something like The Offer into your company, but that's not the goal here.

In research published in 2014, Harris Interactive reported that bad hires had a significant impact on business effectiveness:

- 41% less productivity
- 40% lost time in recruitment
- 37% increase in recruitment costs
- 36% reduction in employee morale in those around the hire

The goal is to look at recruitment as the source of the company brand, rather than an unconnected aspect of your organization. Traditionally, brand is used by HR to promote the recruitment process. In the traditional model, strong brands attract better talent. We need to turn this model on its head and use recruitment to promote the brand.

How can you become more actively involved in the selection process? How can you shape the selection process to choose people who are geared towards your brand objectives?

CULTURE: A LIVING, BREATHING CODE FOR BEHAVIOR

What exactly is corporate culture and why does it lie at the heart of the brand in The Connection Economy?

For many companies, Culture is an intangible aspect of their daily lives. Perhaps there is a rulebook somewhere that enshrines Culture as a list of "do's" and "don'ts". Perhaps there is a list of 10 "values" that you can find on the company website. Perhaps Culture was something candidates studied as a part of their recruitment process but haven't gone back to since.

Rulebooks, value lists and so on - these are not outmoded formats. It's the way we use them that's important. Traditionally, Culture was a monolithic document, or a process driven by an outside consultant, or that thing you did once a year when the team brainstormed values and mission statements on one of those "team-bonding" experience days.

There once was a company that produced a Code of Ethics with the help of a well-known management consultancy. It spoke of corporate responsibility and values like honesty and trust. The Code was written into a 64 page document, handed out to all employees then hung on the lobby walls for visitors and occasional team members to glance at. That was back in 2000 and the company was Enron.

When Zappos CEO Tony Hsieh first floated the idea of company culture he emailed his staff asking for ideas. The result is the dynamic employee handbook. It's 156 pages long, written by the employees themselves and updated daily.

When Culture becomes a museum piece it becomes irrelevant. Employees stray off the path. Culture needs to be a living, breathing entity that all employees are part of in both creating and evolving. Used in this way, culture doesn't become yet another memo to police employees but a powerful touchstone for customer interaction, for marketing and brand experience.

Most companies have a core values statement. Zappos has one too. The key to how this shapes the brand is not in whether you have a statement, but how your people use it and what's actually in it.

Let's take a look at the Zappos list of core values:

i.   Deliver WOW through customer service
ii.   Embrace and drive change
iii.   Create fun and a little weirdness
iv.   Be adventurous, creative and open-minded
v.   Pursue growth and learning
vi.   Build open and honest relationships with communication
vii.   Build a positive team and family spirit
viii.   Do more with less
ix.   Be passionate and determined
x.   Be humble

Some values are interesting - weirdness, family spirit, humble etc. Off the bat, these core values are a useful starting point to scare off the wrong kind of candidate in the recruitment process, but the core values don't stop there.

Zappos core values are also used every day. Here's how:

Weirdness is celebrated in Zappos, starting day 1 in the recruitment process. One question candidates are asked is "how weird are you (on a scale of 1-10)?" This is a unusual recruitment question that may throw some people off. According to Hsieh, the answer to this question is less important than how people react to it. If the candidate sees weird as negative then they'll say things like "well, I work too hard" or "I am obsessive about detail." These are answers which demonstrate a natural conformity that Zappos is trying to weed out. Zappos doesn't want well-qualified robots, but humans capable of interacting and empathizing with customer problems.

"Deliver WOW through customer service" is perhaps the most interesting of Zappos values for a number of reasons. Firstly, it's top of the list. Secondly, it's what differentiates Zappos from the rest. We're not just talking "customer satisfaction" but "WOW!" As we'll discover in this book, there is a big difference between customer satisfaction and WOW in the Connection Economy. And thirdly, most importantly, is how this core value plays out in the lives of Zappos employees. It's all very well expecting your people to give it 110% but how do you actually guarantee that happens day in day out?

Great brands like Zappos, Red Bull and Monster Energy use Culture as a brand's real competitive advantage. As Tony says, "your culture is your brand." You can't touch it, but you can see it through a company's behaviors and output. The role of the leader is to create an environment where your people can do their best, and one that brings your brand's unique culture to life every day.

METRICS: WHAT'S MEASURED GETS DONE

The old McKinsey saying "what's measured gets done" holds true. You can change People and Culture but if you still measure people with the old Metrics, you'll still get the old results. If you want to WOW your customers, you have to measure WOW first.

Zappos asks customers to fill out a service questionnaire called the "Happiness Experience Form" following every interaction.

The Form measures 4 factors on a 100-point scale:

- Did the agent try twice to make a personal emotional connection (PEC)?
- Did they keep the rapport going after the customer responded to their attempt?
- Did they address unstated needs?
- Did they provide a "wow experience"?

In one example, a Zappos agent was trying to help a customer find shoes for a wedding. The agent asked about her location and found out she had a friend who was married in the same place. (Check the boxes on the PEC.) But by measuring the "wow" the agent went the extra mile.

Zappos didn't have the shoe in stock, so the agent looked at four other sites. They didn't have them, either. So, she called a mall, talked to the manager and found a store that had the right pair. She purchased the shoes and personally mailed them to the customer. She received 100 points for that interaction.

Would the agent go that extra mile if she wasn't being measured on WOW? Chances are no, but it's the same person behaving in the same culture. Metrics help your people focus on the goal and direct their energies accordingly. Your people don't work harder, they just work more effectively and this reflects in how your customers experience your brand.

Zappos is a great example of how companies need to build their brands in The Connection Economy. If Zappos were to copy Nokia's model they would focus their brand process outside the business. People, Culture and Metrics would be less important than choice of agency, the official brand story and celebrity.

Nokia is a product and Zappos is a service. Surely, it's easier to create a brand when you have a service? We hear this a lot. In the customer's mind, there is no difference. It all comes down to how they experience your brand. You could be an energy drink brand or an airline.

What matters is not what you *make* for them, but what you *mean* to them. Let's take a look at some more case study examples of brand in The Connection Economy, in particular why emotional context is far more important than physical content.

CAN ZAPPOS CONTINUE TO BUILD A BRAND WORTH TALKING ABOUT?

If you were to measure conversation about a brand and divide it by actual revenues, Zappos would probably rank in the world's top 10. That's not to say Zappos is hype, it's to say that both customers and marketers alike love to talk about Zappos. Will we still be talking about Zappos 5 years from now?

- Zappos operates in a fiercely competitive market but it has the ultimate backing of Amazon, which gives it clout and access to the world's most advanced retail network
- Tony Hsieh continues to drive innovation at the micro level, with the introduction of flat management structures and even Uber-like surge pricing structures for setting pay rates for staff. While his strategies are high risk and may derail the business or create a breeding ground for talent that takes their ideas elsewhere, it's likely that even if Zappos fails in the long term, we will continue to talk about the business and its people as innovators that laid the tracks for the rest of us. Perhaps the Zappos brand will outlive the business.

CHAPTER 5. APPLE: FROM LIKED TO LOVED

❧❧❧❧❧

Apple co-founder - Steve Jobs

A TOOL FOR THE HEART

In Joshua Stern's biographical movie about the life of Steve Jobs, he depicts a scene with a frustrated Jobs trying to explain the groundbreaking Apple II computer to an industry colleague:

"We're talking about the future.

We're working in a market that doesn't even exist yet,"

Jobs yells on the phone.

"What Intel has done for the microprocessor, we are going to do for the home computer [pause]

…How can you not know what I'm talking about?"

In another call he says,

"No ma'am but it runs on a TV monitor.

Like a television set, exactly.

No, it's not a TV set.

It's a personal computer.

Do you own a typewriter?

Imagine combining your typewriter with your television set."

Jobs slams down the phone, falls back onto the grass, and screams in exasperation.

Jobs was a master storyteller and metaphors played a key role in how he communicated technology.

Consider, for example, how he used the imagery in 1984 to depict Apple in the metaphorical context of the creative underdog versus IBM "Big Brother". Consider also when asked to describe the iPod he simply called it,

"A tool for the heart".

THE APPLE IPOD vs THE MICROSOFT ZUNE

Microsoft launched the Zune in 2006 as a direct response to what we'd today call the iPod "classic".

In many aspects, the Zune was the better product. A Gizmodo review from the same year highlighted how, although the two MP3 players were well-balanced in appeal, the Zune triumphed on the important criteria:

- You want a bigger screen? Zune.
- You need an all-you-can-eat subscription service? Zune.
- You want to be different/want something new? Zune.
- Xbox 360 owners who purchase music and want streaming? Zune.
- You want a scratch resistant player? Zune.
- You want a built-in FM tuner? Zune.

Microsoft spent $41 million on marketing the Zune. They had one of the coolest ad agencies in town, Crispin Porter & Bogusky, the same agency that delivered those Microsoft ads with Seinfeld, Bill Gates, Eva Longoria, Deepak Chopra and Pharrell Williams saying "I'm a PC."

So, why *didn't* Microsoft's "iPod killer" kill the iPod? Where the iPod was shifting 10s of millions of units a quarter, the Zune sold only 2 million in the 18 months after its November launch. TIME magazine labeled the Zune one of the "the 10 biggest tech failures of the last decade."

To understand why the iPod beat the Zune we need to view the competition not in terms of their products, you could argue the toss over these, but what lies at the heart their of brand.

"The older I get," said Steve Jobs, "the more I see how much motivations matter. The Zune was crappy because the people at Microsoft don't really love music or art the way we do. We won because we personally love music."

Love is a term rarely used in marketing. "Like", however, is everywhere. We live in an era of Like. Media consultants measure brand these days through the number of Likes on Facebook. Few, though, talk about Love.

Yet, consider the difference. How much effort goes into Liking a brand on Facebook? Very little. You probably have a few dozen pages you liked once that you forget about now. Love, however, is a different level of engagement. You don't camp outside the retail store of a brand you *Like*. You don't recommend a brand just because you *Liked* their Facebook page.

The last point is important. When you Like a Facebook page, there is no risk. But, when you recommend a brand to a friend your reputation is at stake. Imagine you recommend the new Android smartphone to a colleague and the phone keeps crashing. She just spent $500 on the phone on your advice and now she's pissed off. For that reason, you don't recommend a brand unless you *Love* it. You don't recommend a brand unless you're sure it won't let you down. You recommend the brands you have a long-standing, trusted relationship with.

Now, let's go back and see how that actually impacts marketing.

Remember that earlier stat from the Nokia story about young people and smartphones? 81% of young people said they bought their smartphones because of what friends, not what ad agencies, said. That means 81% of young people are learning and experiencing brands based on what their friends are recommending, and they're only recommending brands they love.

In the Connection Economy, if customers Like you be afraid, be very afraid. If customers Like you, you might as well be invisible. People only recommend the brands they Love.

NOKIA vs APPLE: LIKED vs LOVED AGAIN

The iPod gave Apple a beachhead in the handheld device market. It's from this vantage point they were able to confidently launch the iPhone.

2 years after the launch of the iPhone, in 2008, we noticed something interesting. Young people were talking about iPhones in a different way than other handset brands. This was particularly evident in comparing their feelings about Apple and Nokia. (Bear in mind that for the last decade, Nokia had been one of the strongest "youth brands" if not one of the most well-known brands in the world.)

We wanted to quantify these emotions so we devised a survey to measure brand engagement between handset brands and young customers. We asked youth two key questions:

i.   Do you like this brand?
ii.   If you use this brand, would you recommend this brand to a friend?

At first, and because these kind of surveys had rarely been done before, we were concerned that the answers would come back the same, meaning the questions were similar but worded differently. To our surprise, we received markedly different results. The data is quite extensive, so let's just focus on the Nokia:Apple breakdown here:

Liked: Nokia: 72% vs. Apple: 22%

Recommend: Nokia: 35% vs. Apple: 82%

What does this data say?

The results showed that while most young people *Liked* Nokia, few of them *Loved* it. That means they knew about it but weren't recommending it. Put this in the context of that ad agency party at The Punk Club in London to launch the 5800. At the time, and when asked, customers were very "aware" of the Nokia brand. In the context of Ogilvy Era metrics, this was the mark of a job well done; after all, advertising is based on measuring awareness, "top of mind", "brand recall" etc.

Simply being aware of a brand in The Connection Economy is not enough and it often has little bearing on how engaged customers are with the company.

At the time, few people *Liked* Apple but those that did, *Loved* it. Far less people were aware of the Apple brand than Nokia but far more were recommending it. 80% said they would recommend it to a friend.

Consider how this data plays out in the handset market. A large, dominant high-visibility brand controls the lion share of the market. But, in comes a challenger that builds a beachhead of Fans who, one customer at a time, convert rivals into their own vocal advocates. If you use an Apple product you probably use it because of someone in your network who also used one.

Slowly but surely, a small beachhead grows until it comes to dominate the market.

CAN'T BUY ME LOVE

So, how do you create brand Love like Apple?

Getting Likes is easy. We need to be careful of how much value we place on Likes. As with the word "friend", social media has co-opted our language: while it promises to make the process of getting friends and likes easier, it doesn't make those relationships any more valuable. 1 real world friend is still more valuable than 1000 Facebook friends. Similarly, you can buy 1000 Facebook Likes for just $5. It's easy come, easy go.

As the Beatles said, "Can't buy me love."

Love is much harder. You can't buy customer trust and attention anymore. You have to earn it. And, earning it starts *inside* the business. Back to the Heart of the Brand again: People, Culture and Metrics. Apple didn't create a powerful brand through advertising but in how it developed its People, Culture and Metrics. Let's look at how Apple did things differently to other IT companies in its sector.

PEOPLE: BUILD A BEACHHEAD

A key part of Apple's brand strategy has been the ability to focus on a specific group of people.

Consider how Apple grew its brand with Millennial customers. A lot of people talk about Millennials being cheap, difficult to please and fickle in their brand choices. That just goes to show how out-of-touch business research can be. Apple proves that Millennials are anything but.

- Young people aren't influenced by old advertising rules. The industry is saying "it's them, not us" to protect themselves from the poor results and ROI they are producing for clients. 82% of iPod owners globally are below the age of 18. 66% of 8-14 year olds in the US request an iPod as a birthday gift compared to 24% who request a Nintendo DS.
- 96% of US teens have owned at least one iPod by the age of 15. 82% of teens who own an iPhone owned an iPod in the previous 3 years.

20 years ago at universities around the world, Apple computers were owned only by designers, architects and left-handers. Today, Macbooks are the rule rather than the exception. How did this happen?

Walk into any Apple Store in town and you'll find Millennials (and a new generation of pre-teens) gathered around the displays.

Apple started focusing on the youth market back in the 80s and 90s with the introduction of its K-12 education strategy and later the launch of Summer Camps and training in-store to attract young customers. Where competitors would be chasing high-end road warriors, Apple knew that reaching this customer base would take time. Every high-end road warrior was once a teen and emotional engagement with brands starts at a young age. Every iPod owner is more likely to buy a Macbook and an iPhone later in life, but you don't create such a strong Fan base without first making the case for long term investment.

For Apple, that investment is paying off:

- 55% of teens in the US own an iPhone and 65% say that their next smartphone will be an iPhone, compared to 24% who say it will be an Android smartphone.
- 68% of teens own an iPad and 64% say their next tablet will be an iPad, compared to 28% who say it will be an Android tablet.

CULTURE: CHOOSE YOUR METAPHORS WISELY

Calling the iPod a "tool for the heart" is a good example of how Steve Jobs used stories, or more accurately metaphors, to shape the Apple brand. We all understand what a heart is. We understand that it has a certain shape, does certain things and if you don't look after it, you're in trouble. Metaphors are powerful because they encode rules and expectations that guide our behavior.

You can use metaphors to talk about brands too. Waiting in line, security checks, lousy food options. Sounds like an airport? But, no, it's the "happiest place on Earth" - Disney World.

Despite these apparent shortcomings, Fans save up all year. Fans bombard pictures of their selfies taken with Mickey and crew in front of Xmas elves pressed cheek and jowl with millions of others on Christmas Day.

Fans consistently rate Disneyworld as one of the highest customer experiences of any brand in the world.

How is this possible, given airports would typically rate at the opposite end of experience? At airports you are met by security guards. Security guards, by their nature, aren't cuddly individuals who you take selfies with. These employees managing the airport hall are deliberately menacing in appearance. Any form of photography is prohibited.

By contrast, Disney doesn't have security guards or employees, they have *cast members* and their "hall" is a *stage*. They have the same issues. Large numbers of people gathering at a high profile target. Lines. Security threats. How is it that the two organizations can produce profoundly different experiences?

Choice of metaphor.

When you call your customers "guests", as Disney does, you have certain expectations and implied rules to guide your behavior about how you should treat guests:

- You don't frisk guests.
- You don't shout at your guests or brush them off dismissively when they ask for directions.
- Guests are to be cherished and looked after.

Rather than point it out on a map, a Disney cast member will walk you as far as necessary to help you locate a rest room or an attraction with the same care and attention you'd lavish on a guest to your dinner party.

Of course, the TSA (the Transportation Security Administration who greet travelers inbound and outbound at every American airport) will never become Disney cast members. Wishful thinking. Consider these two polar opposites as extremes in a sliding scale of how we create a brand experience. On the one end, passengers. On the other, guests.

Same people. The difference? A word. A metaphor. A story. Consider how companies create Brand Love through their use of metaphors:

- Starbucks: Baristas, not customer service employees or "crew" as they're called in McDonald's
- Zappos: Family, not department
- Disney World: Cast, not employees
- Apple: Genius, not customer service reps

Remember that 85% of our brand is defined by how customers interact with it on an everyday basis. Metaphors make a profound difference to the brand because they encode the behaviors we expect of our people. Brand starts right here on the inside of the company in its own Culture.

Choose your metaphors wisely.

Here's one more to consider.

In a bedroom somewhere in the world right now, there is a teenager standing in front of the mirror with a tennis racquet or hair brush pretending to be Justin Bieber, Jimmy Page, Bibi Zhou or Jay Chou. What creates this enduring love for musicians?

It's not because they're famous. We don't hold the same feelings about Barack Obama, David Cameron or Francois Hollande even though these names are perhaps more famous in their respective countries. The difference is how they engage us and it's also a good metaphor for understanding how we interact with customers – are we like Politicians or Musicians? Your choice of metaphor shapes everything.

Take a look at how Politicians interact with voters:

Politicians need 51% of the vote to win. Politicians don't need people to Love them, they just need to be Liked more than the next guy. They take every photo opportunity with army veterans, toddlers and wheel-chaired voters. They appear on camera with a carefully cherry picked audience of faces behind them that represent the exact demographic mix of their audience. Everything is stage-managed not to offend. When politicians like Mitt Romney let slip how they really feel about the masses while still on mic, all hell breaks loose. It's a career that attracts those who are capable of playing the game: being everything to everybody.

It takes hundreds of millions of dollars to elect a politician these days, sums which carry huge compromises in values and beliefs. That's why we Like them but find it difficult to trust them.

Musicians, however, don't play that game. Sure, there are those who play the game like politicians, selling out their craft to appease the record label, but those that survive long term are the musicians who are unapologetic in their message. The most successful musicians are true to their heart.

Look at the best-selling musicians of all time alive today:

- Paul McCartney/Ringo Starr from the Beatles
- Madonna
- Elton John
- Led Zeppelin
- Pink Floyd

Here's a list of artists who have openly courted controversy in their views on politics, sexuality and drug use. Were they apologetic? No. When you're true to your heart, you don't compromise. No politician would ever survive doing the things musicians claim they did. If a politician smokes a joint, we go stir crazy, turning it into an international incident. Yet, when musicians do it, it hardly raises an eyebrow.

Take a look at those top 5 artists again. That's over 2 billion record sales between them. They sell because they have a beachhead of Fans who Love what they do. Musicians don't need to spend hundreds of millions of dollars promoting their message because the marketing's baked into their Fanbase. It's these Fans who line up to get the first concert tickets, buy every album and tell their friends.

The reason why Psy (of Gangnam Style fame) will never feature in this list is because he doesn't have the Fan base these musicians have. Remember all that hype surrounding his video? 1 billion views. The fact he met Obama in the White House is telling. Where are the people talking about Psy now?

Marketing is no longer about getting elected. You don't need 51% of the market to win in The Connection Economy. You don't need to stage manage your message to avoid offense. Find the Fans who Love you and do everything you can to delight and "wow" them.

METRICS: MEASURE LOVE, NOT LIKE

You can't create Brand Love with the metrics of Like or Awareness. No matter how much you stand up on stage and bang the drum on "engaging the customer" or "capturing their hearts and minds", what counts is the metrics.

Apple focuses on metrics that encourage customer Love (NPS: Net Promoter Score). As Jobs himself said, they'd rather capture a "share of customer" than a "share of market." Consider the Nokia vs Apple example earlier. If you measure and reward Like as your marketing goal, you will achieve a result like Nokia:

- Mass brand awareness
- "top of mind"
- Many likes

When we look at these metrics we see a whole host of brands like Samsung, Sony, Pepsi, McDonald's and Microsoft using this old model. But how resilient is this strategy to competition? All it takes is a highly focused, Loved brand to erode your customer base one person at a time.

NPS is a metric widely used by brands mentioned in this book. NPS is measured by asking customers to rate the brand on a score of 1-10 based on how likely they would be to recommend it to a friend. The next time you buy or get something fixed at the Apple Store, look out for the message that will land in your email box several days later. It will ask you an NPS based question.

A lot of companies use NPS but the key difference between the brands in this book and everybody else is how they use it. There is a big difference between using NPS to measure customer satisfaction and using it as a starting point for activity.

In most companies, NPS is used as a vanity metric: a score like customer satisfaction that gets attention when it's good and buried when it's not. Companies use vanity metrics to pat themselves on the back. Often business analysts gather the numbers, silo them in their department and then publish them on a quarterly or annual basis. Sometimes external agencies do this job.

This is what we call a Net Promoter Score. What Apple has, however, is a Net Promoter *System*. Rather than feed your post-retail store interaction back to a pool of bean counters, the number goes straight to the Frontline. Everyday, Apple Genius employees go through what they call "the daily download" - a team meeting where they download the latest NPS data.

Imagine what the System does for Frontline staff. Staff not only have immediate feedback on their activity but they also have a starting point for what to do next. You have a *feedback loop* that creates fast turnarounds, bypassing corporate bureaucracy. If that in-store promotion worked, do more of that. If that in-store training failed, do less of that. It's simple mechanics that define the brand on an everyday basis and it starts with focusing on measuring Love, not Like.

CAN APPLE CONTINUE TO BUILD A BRAND WORTH TALKING ABOUT?

It's very difficult and often unwise to call out an apparent shortcoming in Apple's strategy. They have an uncanny ability to beat expectations and silence critics with results and products that set new benchmarks in an increasingly wider scope of industries.

Will we continue to talk about Apple in 5 years' time or will Apple become the next Nokia or Kodak? Difficult to say with its ventures into new sectors like watches, TV and automotive. Most sensible management wisdom would warn of overstretch but, as said, Apple has a history of tearing up the rule books when it comes to management wisdom.

There are a few worrying signs, however, indicative of a brand that's topped its market:

- *Apple is substantially increasing its paid media spend. While Apple is nowhere near spending as much as its nearest rival, Samsung, it has doubled its ad spend in the last 2 years. This data suggests one of two things: a) Apple's revenues have grown so fast ad spend hasn't kept pace or b) Apple is becoming increasingly impatient with driving long term relationships. As a standalone data point, little can be gleaned from the growth, so we need to see it in context of other changes.*
- Jobs and Johnson no longer steer the Apple ship so, in that respect, it has lost 2 of its key business drivers. Not saying that Tim Cook's team is any less capable but they may have a different vision for Apple that Jobs and Johnson laid out. One such point of difference is the role of the store. The launch of the Apple Watch demonstrates how stores are becoming less an experience and place for education, more the sharp end of sales.

Apple has a lot of customer and industry goodwill built over the last 20 years. What Apple does today, good or bad, will continue to yield results. Pivoting from earned media to paid media will yield short term results which will please the market, but Apple will effectively be cashing in on the lump sum in its goodwill bank account rather than living off the interest. In time, the truth will bear out.

CHAPTER 6. LEGO: PUT FANS AT THE HEART OF THE BRAND

᪐᪐᪐᪐᪐

Lego Brand Fan - Alice Finch

FIND YOUR FANS

"I will NOT show this to my daughter! She saved her allowance for close to a year to be able to afford the full official Hogwarts castle lego set, bless her. Seeing this might fuel an obsession we might not be able to handle..." said one commenter.

"Fantastic!"

"Just saw this in person at ECCC and it was absolutely mind-blowing! The detail is INSANE."

"Wow this is just incredibly awesome!"

"That is ridiculously amazing. Kudos to such a cool, creative mom!"

"WOW!! My lego mad seven year old wants to go live with her....and the lego!!!"

"Oh I'm such a Harry Potter geek, this is amazing!!!!!"

You are reading the feedback to what the Kotaku website says "...might be the most impressive LEGO construction ever made by a single person."

It's a near-perfect replica build on Harry Potter Hogwarts using LEGO bricks.

400,000 bricks.

It's the work of Alice Finch, a self-confessed LEGO and Harry Potter Fan who spent 2 years creating the build, losing 2 fingerprints on her index fingers and picking up knee injuries and various bouts of RSI in the process.

"It sounds odd to say 'LEGO-related injuries' but it is possible," she told the media.

"I had invested a tremendous amount of effort (and money) into it because I loved building my own bit of reality for the world of Harry Potter and because I wanted my kids to be able to play in all the spaces where the story takes place, but I didn't really think about how others would view it. Enormous perhaps, but beyond that, I just didn't know."

Finch's Hogwarts won the People's Choice and Best in Show awards at the Seattle-based BrickCon Convention last fall. It was shown again at Seattle's Emerald City Comicon. Children and parents alike stop and admire the structure and gawp at this testament to a Fan's dedication.

Her journey into the world of Harry Potter started 15 years ago with the release of the first book in her early 20s. Since then she's bought every book and watched every movie. It's a journey without a seeming destination but it's a constant in her life. When her children were old enough to help, sharing the stories and working on LEGO bricks together became a common bond with her family.

"I haven't built since I was a kid and once I started building again, it occurred to me that building with my son had important implications," said Finch in an interview with a LEGO enthusiast website. "We were spending time together doing something creative, learning techniques and sharing ideas in a very productive way, and, although I didn't really think about it at the time, I was showing him that moms can be pretty darn good at putting bricks together too."

"When I could, I'd build during the day with my two boys in the LEGO room, doing things like building the layer upon layer of the now even bigger central tower that would accommodate moving staircases and portraits in the walls. I was pretty tired of course after months of staying up late, but I think adrenaline kept me going. I just had to finish and so I kept working until I did.

"My older son likes setting up scenes so he posed many of the hundreds of students and professors all over the castle. My younger son helped by testing the sturdiness of the buildings, the usability of the classrooms, and he contributed several charmingly wobbly shrubs down by Hagrid's hut.

"My husband helped where he could with things like the conical roofs (which were drat tricky to build), the harp in the room with Fluffy, giving a second opinion here and there, but mostly he helped by reading to me while I worked. That and never flinching at the enormous number of bricks that kept arriving by the box and oozing into all the rooms of the house."

For the true Fan, there is no consideration of cost or time; it's a labor of Love. Building Hogwarts from memory wasn't enough. She had to travel to locations in the movie from Seattle to Oxford in England because she "wanted to build a more architecturally accurate version".

"I went to the Harry Potter studio tour in London to see the sets in person," said Seattle resident, Alice Finch.

"This was tremendously helpful because some sets are only shown from certain angles and seeing them in person meant I could fill in the gaps and take hundreds of photos from all angles. They even had a room full of the architectural drawings! The last room had the model they built for all the wide shots for everything but the last films. It was quite a sight as it was enormous and meant I could get my own photos of panoramas and small architectural details."

When a company talks about "fans", they often mean people who Like their Facebook page. Once again, like the word "friend" and "like" itself, social media has co-opted the language of relationships. Alice Finch is no "fan". That's why we're talking about Fans with a capital "F". These are the true Fans of your brand you need to seek out, not the Likers on Facebook, because it's these customers who are a powerful asset in your marketing.

This is exactly what LEGO did, and this is how it built one of the most successful brands of the modern era.

THE LEGO BRAND TURNAROUND

LEGO CEO Jorgen Knudstorp

LEGO is a brand today that stands alongside Coke, Starbucks and Nike in terms of global recognition. Parents from Mumbai to New York could opt for cheaper, imitation Chinese blocks but they choose LEGO - a brand synonymous with trust.

Such is its global appeal that experts estimate there are 60 LEGO bricks in circulation for every one of the world's inhabitants. LEGO sells 7 sets every second, crafting 36,000 pieces every minute of every day. Children spend 5 billion hours a year playing with those bricks. LEGO movies, LEGO fan clubs, LEGO Harry Potter, Star Wars and so on. LEGO bears the hallmarks of a strong brand on the rise.

But it wasn't always this way. By the turn of the 90s it looked like LEGO's adherence to tradition was beginning to make the brand look old and out of touch. A new generation of consumers were buying games consoles, computers, later iPads and mobile phones. 20 years ago, LEGO was in serious decline. Plastic bricks looked dated. LEGO theme parks and the computer games subsidiary were leaking money.

In response, LEGO sought out innovative ideas from new blood. Management axed many lifelong LEGO employees and sought out award-winning talent from Europe's most prestigious design schools. New designers brought new ideas but few of these were founded on what customers actually wanted. Designers spent most of their time designing, not "out there" talking to Fans like Alice Finch. New design school recruits became overly-concerned with the ethics and aesthetics of design.

In short, LEGO lost touch.

"People had personal relationships with elements," said design director Dorthe Kjaerulff, referring to LEGO's vast inventory of pieces (or "elements" as LEGO employees call them). Staff would regularly fight corners to protect their own elements, for fear of losing territory or opening up their silos. One protracted discussion involved the fate of a LEGO figurine chef who was traditionally produced in 2 varieties - one with and one without mustache. It was a debate that took up countless hours. Reformers wanted to save money by producing only one figure, but stubborn designers wouldn't budge, feeling their ideas (and purpose) was under attack. Eventually, the mustache-less chef was axed.

Products like Znap, Primo, Scala and Galidor - products which now fade into history - all emerged from this dark, insular, design-driven period in LEGO's history. Galidor was LEGO's attempt at creating a full range of innovative products including Power-Rangers-like action figures with their own ecosystem of accessories. LEGO bet on cross-marketing with retailers (Galidor Happy Meals at McDonald's), a TV show, video games and DVDs as key to pushing the range out to prospective buyers. But LEGO's bet failed. They misjudged the customer. The TV show fared poorly. One anonymous executive said he was "gobsmacked with disgust" as they watched their designs sink into anonymity. A year later, the range was gone.

LEGO's problem lay in its product-first focus. A lack of focus on what customers did with these bricks was driving a long term slide into irrelevance. Rather than look at what customers wanted, much of what came out of LEGO HQ was guesswork. When LEGO decided to expand into a new range of licensed box sets, they faced an uphill struggle. According to one source, the decision to license the Star Wars franchise in 1999 was easy in comparison to the internal struggle management faced in having a product with the word "War" in the title.

Being product-focused also meant costs spiraled out of control. The average set inventory grew from 6,000 to 12,000 parts. When machine molds for each part cost 50,000 Euros ($45,000) to produce, storage and production costs spiraled out of control. Many sets were making a loss before they hit the shelves.

By the turn of the millennium, LEGO management were faced with a dilemma. LEGO announced record losses of $400 million. Such was the scale of their decline that the company had to either do the unthinkable: declare bankruptcy or initiate radical change.

If LEGO was going to change, it would need to first change its people and that would start with the CEO. Enter Jorgen Vig Knudstorp - a management consultant who learned his craft working for McKinsey. He was an outsider, unconnected to the LEGO family that ran the business for the best part of a century. Aged 36, with only 3 years of service at LEGO, he was the disruptive force that Chairman Kristiansen felt the company needed. In 2001, Knudstorp took over the reins with a mandate to affect radical change and save the company.

We'll talk about LEGO's turnaround in the context of the Heart of the Brand: People, Culture and Metrics. But first, let's look at the numbers. Did it work?

Consider that LEGO was $400m in debt and facing bankruptcy. LEGO was losing money on every set produced and operating with spiraling production costs.

Today, following Knudstorp's reforms, LEGO is not just in a different place, but a different world entirely:

- Return on equity increased from zero in 2004 to 70% 10 years later.
- LEGO grew its market cap from 400 million Danish Krone to 11 billion today (a 25 fold increase over a decade). If LEGO were listed on NASDAQ, experts value the company at around $150 billion.

Behind this success story lay a more effective and efficient LEGO. And it's a story built on people like Alice Finch who LEGO calls AFOLs (Adult Fans of LEGO). In reconnecting with the heart of the market rather than ideas about design, LEGO managers were able to slice development time in half on new products to 12 months. LEGO became more targeted. Gone was the guesswork and blue sky pontification and in its place, hard data and powerful insight that guided decision-making.

LEGO grew its marketing ROI and customer loyalty:

- Gross margins grew from 56% to 70%.
- Operating costs fell from 70% to 37% of turnover.
- Employees, too, became more productive: sales per employee doubled in 6 years.

10 years ago, the dominant toy brand Mattel could have crushed LEGO but today the tables have turned. In 2014, LEGO passed Mattel to become the most valuable toy brand in the world. It's Mattel who's now struggling. Where LEGO nurtured Fans at the heart of its brand, Mattel resorted to buying them:

"Mattel acquires key adult LEGO fan sites to convert AFOLs to AFOMs" - Brickset headline, April 2014.

PEOPLE: START WITH YOUR FANS

Knudstorp built the LEGO brand on people, in particular its own Fans, and how they interacted with the brand on a daily basis. Core to Knudstorp's turnaround was a reconnection with the heart of LEGO's brand: play.

Leg Godt: Danish for play well.

Knudstorp needed to remind his people that their children, and their children's children would both need and enjoy play, as had our forebears. And in this legacy, LEGO could continue to thrive.

"[Children] still want to have that physical LEGO building experience that cannot be replaced by digital play," said Knudstorp in an interview with Monocle magazine.

It was a sentiment reflected worldwide. As news of LEGO's impending doom or potential takeover by predatory venture firms filtered out to the public, countless parents wrote direct to Chairman Kristiansen with one simple message: "Please, for God's sake, save this brand because we love it so much."

Many doubted the future of an analog toy that seemed at odds with the demands of the digital age. Yet, Knudstorp reminded his people to look at books and music. Analysts had long forecast how technology would sweep away these "dead wood" legacies of the analog age but they defied every prognosis, coming back stronger than ever.

The story could have played out differently. A brand makeover, a relaunch, a focus on integrating LEGO with tablets and smartphones. We'd be talking about creative agencies and Big Ideas in the spirit of Levi's or California Raisins.

But times have changed. No longer can brands be cosmetically redefined from the outside; they have to be re-engineered at the Heart of the business. On the inside were the Fans like Alice Finch, which LEGO took to the heart of its business.

Forget the brand makeover, real turnarounds start inside the business with your People. In the Connection Economy, brands are built on people and the most important people are your Fans - both employees and customers.

Earlier we looked at how Zappos used recruitment as a key starting point for defining its brand. Apple does the same although we'll look at that in a later section. For LEGO, too, recruitment is an important element of the marketing strategy.

If you want to nurture your brand Fans, the process starts with your recruitment for 2 reasons:

i.   Focus on recruiting Fans
ii.   Focus on recruiting people who can connect with Fans

Finding your Fans isn't an external process that can be solved by an agency, but one that reflects who you are recruiting and how those people interact with your market.

To understand its brand truth "Play", Knudstorp needed to connect with those people *playing* with their products, to create a Culture that encouraged *play* and metrics that rewarded it.

On the inside, LEGO had to change its people. Knudstorp axed many of the old school designers who LEGO recruited in the 90s to make way for Fans of the brand. Engineers were recruited less on the basis of which school they went to and their design philosophies and more on their passions for the LEGO.

Too many professionals pay a lot of money to get their MBAs to sit in a big chair in the corner office. What a waste. Watch marketers like Zappos CEO Tony Hsieh man the call center telephones or Rodney Sacks, CEO of Monster, out there interacting with Fans at action sports events or LEGO CEO Jorgen Knudstorp taking part in LEGO Brick Cons with other enthusiasts. In all these examples, you'll see that real brand leadership isn't set in manuals or memos, but through example.

Like many manufacturers, LEGO suffered from a product-focused culture. That had to change. Knudstorp needed to put Fans, people like Alice Finch at the heart of the brand and create a culture that amplified their voice.

By walking the shop floor and talking to Fans, Knudstorp led by example. He spent as little time in the office as possible. By stepping out of the weekly sales management and capacity allocation meetings, Knudstorp began to reinforce cultural change. No longer would decisions be the preserve of their 12 VPs and the hierarchical matrix structure, but be part and parcel of every manager's daily life regardless of title.

Managers would soon learn what customers wanted and, importantly, which products were making money and which weren't. Rather than writing memos or holding meetings with senior management, managers were out there talking to factory workers, downloading insights from retailers or connecting with fans at LEGO conventions.

Knudstorp needed people who felt comfortable talking to employees on the factory floor, to engineers and marketers rather than corporate climbers who hid behind their corporate titles and MBAs. And he needed people who could act on these gut instincts. Management began to value their time talking to customer service teams. No longer were they a cost center that deflected complaints, as is the case in so many companies today, but an emerging goldmine of LEGO insight.

Knudstorp calls LEGO's closeness to the customer the "avenue of truth". That truth isn't held in the brand management document, the focus group of the creative agency Big Idea, but in what the grassroots customers, Fans and retailers say about the product. If LEGO Fans don't like a product, they'll tell you. If they want new features, they'll tell you too. You just have to give them a voice and deliver on the promise that their voice will make a difference.

"Nine out of ten times [customers] may tell you something you know or something you consider vaguely relevant, but if you dismiss those nine times you never get the tenth time where they tell you something that's really, really crucial and you were never aware of. If they didn't tell you maybe you'd only learn two, three years later, and then of course it's too late," said Knudstorp.

By contrast, pre-Knudstorp LEGO didn't know how far off track it was. There were few lines of communication. Managers rarely talked to customers and decisions were made on ideas learned from business school texts rather than conversations with fans.

CULTURE: GIVE FANS A VOICE

Fans are an important part of the marketing mix because they are replacing the role traditionally held by market gatekeepers. That means Fans are the new influencers, the new routes to the market, the new advertising.

Let's look at the 4 ways Fans power up your marketing mix:

i.   Fans are the influencers
ii.   Fans are the brand custodians
iii.   Fans are the early adopters
iv.   Fans are the creators

1) Fans are the influencers. Fans aren't 2 or 3 times more influential than the average customer, but up to 100 times more influential. Fans are the 10% that influence the 90%. The 90% aren't listening to you anyway, just tuning into their peers. It's Fans that encourage them to switch mobile phone brands. It's Fans that give them reasons to leave a service. It's Fans that educate them about new products.

2) Fans are the brand custodians. Fans will defend your brand. They won't switch just because the next guy is cheaper, better or cooler. Fans switch when you piss them off. When DC Comics gave readers the option to choose their own endings, people voted to kill off Robin in the Batman series. Although Robin's death raised issues of the series' longevity and was chosen by popular vote, Fans ardently voted against it.

Customers wanted to kill off Robin because it was "fun" and "different", but Fans who cared about the Batman series wanted him to stay. DC killed him off only to realize later on they made a mistake, and they reversed the decision. Customers don't necessarily care about the brand long term because they have nothing to lose.

3) Fans are the early adopters. They are the first to try out new products, the most honest with feedback and the most forgiving of your failures if you treat them with respect.

4) Fans are the creators. When marketing departments go to bed at night, Fans are carrying the torch relentlessly. They're updating web content, creating YouTube videos and putting stickers on their bikes. In terms of sheer numbers, you cannot compare traditional marketing with the power of Fans. Kodak can only run a handful of marketing campaigns at any one time yet GoPro has over 50 million video homages on YouTube, 99% of which are from Fans.

If you don't know who your Fans are, you only have customers.

LEGO works hard to give Fans the platforms and tools they need to connect with each other and share their conversations with the company. LEGO ideas is one such strategy to join the dots, a platform to source Fan ideas and conversations:

Have an idea for a LEGO set?

i.   Share your idea
ii.   Gather support
iii.   LEGO review
iv.   New LEGO product

Ready to get started?

For LEGO Fans, it's a tantalizing prospect: turn your crazy dreams into reality. LEGO Ideas is a crowdsourcing platform for LEGO fan ideas where fans can vote on their own projects. LEGO selects and reviews the best projects with a view to developing commercial prototypes.

The LEGO Lightsaber is an idea submitted by Scott34567 on the LEGO Ideas website. The Lightsaber has over 1,000 fan comments and more than 10,000 upvotes. Once ideas hit 10K, LEGO stops counting but at that point they are selected for official consideration.

There are over 8000 Fan-submitted projects still in the voting stage (or "gathering support" as Ideas calls it).

Projects range from color sudoku to a replica Neuschwanstein castle. It's not just about submitting ideas, it's about creating conversations. With each project there is discussion. Fans from other websites pour in to support and bump up their causes. As Fans take their conversations off-site they influence others to get involved. Fans debate technicalities like what should and shouldn't feature in the sets. Should Minecraft Creepers have bigger heads? How do you best recreate an underwater Geodesic dome with LEGO bricks? How does LEGO best represent a Minecraft Zombie, or even a floating or invisible element? It's almost as if the design and purchase of the product is secondary to the conversation about it.

Exceptional brands join the dots. They create platforms to connect Fans with each other. Once you connect Fans, you create a powerful experience; you become unmissable. You become part of their Ecosystem. You stick around. Engaging Fans isn't about sending the right messages into the market but identifying what's stopping the market and the organization interacting on natural terms.

Rather than ask "how do we engage our Fans?" we need to be asking, "how do we break down the walls that prevent those Fans from engaging us?"

METRICS: MEASURE LOYALTY, NOT SHORT TERM SALES

The LEGO story is about defining brand in your People and Culture. But, Metrics are important too. It might surprise you to learn that great brands like LEGO and Apple don't reward their employees on sales. It seems almost unconscionable that modern companies can expect great sales without tying in their people to the top line somehow, but that's how these brands do differently. Neither offer sales commission.

"Nobody at LEGO is measured on sales because the most important thing is that kids and retailers return for more in future." - Jorgen Knudstorp, CEO LEGO.

By contrast, LEGO measures repeat business and customer loyalty. And that's what it gets.

LEGO bases manager bonuses, including Knudstorp's, on customer satisfaction surveys of retailers, parents and children. This is supposed to ensure the brand's long-term health is never sacrificed for short-term financial success.

If you want to nurture Fans you need the right Metrics at the heart of the process. Without changing the metrics, you'll always end up with the same result: customers.

BONUS CASE STUDY: FORD

Revitalizing the prospects of mega-brands like LEGO can appear daunting. But if you take small steps, as long as your direction is correct, you'll steer the whole company towards a better direction.

Ford is a great example of this:

- Ford went from being at the precipice of bankruptcy in 2008 to launching one of the top 10 coolest auto brands 3 years later.
- No makeover, no re-launch, no new agency.
- Ford did it all by going back to basics and focusing on Brand Love.

Ford is a useful case study to reinforce the case for building on Brand Love. There is a long established precedent in automotive marketing. Here are some of the world's biggest advertisers so to simply choose to do anything but advertising in this sector is radical in itself. A year doesn't pass without one auto brand trying to out-advertise its rival at the Super Bowl. Auto has a well-worn track of building buzz: inviting journalists & celebrities, buying spots on TV, product placement in movies and auto show reveals. It's safe, comfortable and boring.

Ford, like LEGO, needed to do different.

Before the turnaround, Ford was in trouble. Their problems didn't lie in having a poor product line but in the long-term alienation of Fans. Employees drove Ford. Employee families and friends drove Ford. Employees lived in towns where everyone either drove the brand or worked for a company that supplied it. When young people started buying cooler Japanese marques, Ford couldn't understand why its brand was suddenly uncompetitive.

By 2008, stock prices fell to $1.50. Ford was finished long before the recession ever hit.

Rather than seek answers with its ad agency, Ford looked to its community, its tribe of customers who stuck with them despite the downturn. Ford turned to established networks like SEMA (the special equipment manufacturers association) where the most dedicated and die-hard enthusiasts can be found. Ford knew that if it was going to influence the mass market, it needed to start at the core, the fans who hang out at SEMA, who modified cars, who talked about the brand even when traditional marketers were ignoring them.

By identifying and co-creating with the fans who loved their products, particularly American students who were already sold on the brand, Ford manage to slowly turn the juggernaut 'round. Rather than try to impress them with cool marketing campaigns, Ford realized that students had a lot to offer – from their ideas about fuel efficiency in the face of rising oil prices to the future roadmap for mobile phone / car integration. By creating a movement – the Ford Fiesta movement – Ford began to treat youth as partners in the whole process. Sure, students couldn't actually design new models but they could help co-create the stories around the cars and share innovative ideas about in-car entertainment or safety.

"We didn't want A-list celebrities. We know that people trust people like themselves most, and our agents are a good representation of many of the people we're interested in reaching. Plus, they all wanted to be part of this - we didn't have to go out and hire them," said Scott Monty, Head of Social Media for Ford Motor Company.

Ford extended an open invitation to find young people who would be interested in borrowing a Fiesta for six months. At the end of the six months, one of them would receive a brand new Ford Fiesta. Over 4,000 people applied to become part of the

Fiesta Movement. Ford accepted 100 of them and made them "Agents."

Ford followed their everyday stories, curated the content and gave it a home online. Agents created video shorts, documented their travels, discovered little-known places, interviewed interesting people - one of them even used the car to elope. Very few of the pictures taken and videos created were about the Fiesta itself. Those that did just showed the car briefly - around 3 seconds in a 5-minutes video.

Agents weren't asked to talk about the car or the brand, they asked them to talk about themselves. In fact if you looked at the agent's page on the Ford Fiesta Movement website you struggle to see any evidence of the Ford logo or brand. It wasn't about the car, after all. It was about the people, not "can you make the logo bigger?"

Ford didn't even ask the Agents to put their videos on the Fiesta Movement webpage; because these students were the type that loved to perform anyway (talk, write, act, sing, create movies) it was second nature. These hopefuls needed Ford's platform to tell their story and Ford needed them to generate the fans it required to shape their target market. It was an approach that required a degree of confidence in the new brand model and a departure from the ubiquitous "go social" attitude offered by creative agencies.

"The whole process has been very organic, warm and fuzzy, and not at all pushy or forced," said Maria De Los Angeles, Agent#27. "I'm not a 'money' person and I have no idea if this will help Ford's bottom line in the end when it comes to selling cars but I can tell you that from professional perspective that this has got to be one of the most brilliant campaigns ever. It fully engages us as ambassadors without us being hardcore salespeople. We are not required to yap about the Fiesta constantly and we can pretty much say whatever we want. The only thing we're not allowed to do in our videos is shoot something stupid — i.e., driving without a seat belt, that sort of thing. Ford took a great risk in putting these cars in our hands."

Ford gave them a stage, a car for half a year and helped them do what they've always loved doing. The Fiesta Movement was not an overnight success. The program started long before the first car hit the dealerships.

By working with Fans, Ford primed the market, reducing the risk of a cold-start come launch day. Behind the scenes, Ford also opened up other opportunities for co-creation. University hackathons much like those hosted by Facebook challenged students to develop the kind of driving apps they wanted to see in their own cars. The best apps were taken forward (official or not) for in-car development, such as the SyncML Spotify app that allows the driver to play streaming music straight out of the car speakers from his or her music playlist. Not only was this co-creation great innovation, it was also great marketing. Product development and marketing became one virtuous cycle fueled by Fan love.

CAN LEGO CONTINUE TO BUILD A BRAND WORTH TALKING ABOUT?

LEGO continues to go from strength to strength, defying analyst expectations and ideas about what's possible for an analog toy brand in the digital world.

In this scenario, we'd be worried if brand leaders became impatient and began ratcheting up the paid media spend to keep pace with investor expectations or maintain the market buzz. But, being privately held, LEGO has a distinct advantage - it can keep the business focused on longer term needs. We're not saying privately held companies are better, because strong management wins over investors every time, but it's a lot easier to do it when the CEO and CMO aren't constantly pandering to the short term needs of the market.

So far, LEGO appears committed to its Fan base, which is an encouraging sign for long term growth. With an army of Fans, LEGO keeps cheaper imitators out. But, there are concerns that LEGO should be mindful of:

- *LEGO needs to ensure the success of its high visibility franchises (e.g. Star Wars and Harry Potter) doesn't crowd out management focus on Fans and platforms like Lego Ideas, ReBrick etc.*
- Success can often create marketing echo chambers. Like any megastar of the pop world, success attracts its own coterie of sycophants who shield people from the real world. "Keeping it real" is exactly how LEGO turned around its brand so it's critical to maintain a culture where managers are expected to invest time in the Frontline and "get out there". When the LEGO marketing department building is full on any given afternoon, the brand has peaked.

CHAPTER 7. MONSTER ENERGY DRINKS: BUILDING A BRAND WITHOUT COMPROMISE

ശശശശശ

Monster Truck Driver - Tyler M.

BRAND IS PEOPLE

A matte-black, jacked up Chevrolet Silverado with 18" wide Nitto Grappler All Terrain Tires and green claw decal dominates the parking lot. Angry metal music blasts from the grille speakers. A giant figure of Beyoncé beams down over the parking lot of the stadium brandishing a Pepsi can in one hand. 50 feet below, dozens of ant-sized people stream out of their cars towards the stadium entrance.

Under the gaze of this improbably beautiful siren, a thin white tattooed leg dangles from of the truck parked outside the main entrance. He pushes the truck door open and is soon swamped by a crowd of teens. They peer inside. One pair poses behind the rear tailgate and takes a selfie. Two more join. The driver decamps and begins handing out cans and stickers to the eager teens. Some also pose for selfies with the driver at the front of the truck.

The truck driver, Tyler, doesn't look much older than the teens he's surrounded by. They pester him for something. He reaches into the dash with his long, thin, tattooed arm and rummages around trinkets and soda cans to pull out a pile of Monster logo caps. The mob intensifies around the driver. They all want one.

With his ink and piercings, he probably wouldn't stand much of chance in the traditional advertising or marketing world. He'd need a lot of scrubbing up before you took him home to meet your mom and he would look out of place in most offices. He's the kind of person that brands like Pepsi would sweep under the carpet when they roll out the welcome for Beyoncé. He's the uncomfortable truth. But this isn't about fitting in. Tyler isn't about compromise. Maybe that's because Tyler spends only one day a month in the office. The rest of the time he is out there - talking to the market.

To most brands, Tyler is just a regular employee. He's one of the grunts that make the operations tick over, slavishly putting in the hours driving up and down the California coast to deliver cans of Monster Energy Drinks to retailers or hand them out at events. But, to the company, Monster, he's an important brand touchpoint. When teens crowd round Tyler's truck all bets about previous ad campaigns are off. How many of those teens are thinking about that giant Beyoncé billboard now? You probably forgot too.

Monster is a multi-billion dollar brand. At times it's been more profitable per employee than Apple. Monster has grown its market share from nothing to a market lead of 36% of the US market, bigger than nearest rival and heavy-spender Red Bull. And it's achieved this with zero advertising. At the heart of Monster's brand was a conscious commitment to grow its Fan base without advertising.

Traditional Ogilvy-Era marketing focuses on resource intensive launches e.g. media buying, expensive campaigns and in-store promotions. This approach produces a tangible but very short-lived spike. By contrast, Monster focuses 100% on the target market and not wasting a single cent of their marketing budget on celebrities or ad campaigns. All resources are invested in converting the target market into Fans, who then go on to influence and recruit mainstream customers.

By focusing on the long term, Monster has become the #1 energy drink in the US and continues this trend across the world without spending a dollar on traditional advertising.

It's what Jamal Benmiloud, ex VP of marketing for Monster calls "story making" rather than "story telling", building the brand from the inside, starting with its own people, growing an authentic brand. Fans tattoo the Monster claw on their bodies, apply decals to their bikes and paint it on their cars. Wherever you experience Monster, people feel the authenticity.

The success of Monster's brand has never been about their ability to pay for a clever media agency (they don't use them) but their ability to get the right people on board and to leverage those people's own networks to create influence within the markets they were targeting. That meant hiring people like Tyler, not because he knew about marketing or advertising in the traditional sense, but because he could connect with the target audience at the Frontline in a meaningful way. And wherever there is MotoCross, BMX, punk rock concerts, drift, mountain biking, surfing or NASCAR, wherever there are fans gathering, there are Monster trucks diligently building the brand, one customer at a time.

"Most companies spend their money on ad agencies, TV commercials, radio spots, and billboards to tell you how good their products are. Instead, we support the scene, our bands, our athletes and our fans!

At Monster, all of our guys walk the walk in action sports, punk rock music, partying, hangin' with the girls, and living life on the edge. Monster is way more than an energy drink. Led by our athletes, musicians, employees, distributors and fans, Monster is a lifestyle in a can!"
- from Monster Energy official Facebook page.

THE PEPSI GENERATION, THE BIG IDEA AND THE OLD SODA MODEL OF MARKETING

To understand what lies at the heart of Monster's Brand success we need to understand where it came from. We're not talking about the brand's origins but more the industry in which it operates - soda.

Soda marketing has produced perhaps some of the most iconic, if not expensive, marketing in the world. We can all recall a Pepsi or a Coke ad from our childhood. The reason? Soda. What differentiates one soda from the next guy? Nothing. They're all just fizzy, colored water. When your product offers no point of difference, it all comes down to the marketing. Soda is the pinnacle of marketing because marketing is 100% of the reason soda brands succeed or fail.

But that doesn't mean all soda brands are good at it. It just means the premium on soda marketing is a lot higher than other sectors. Contrast Monster's approach with Pepsi, for example, and you see that strategies vary widely. Unlike Monster, Pepsi is built the traditional way, from the outside, with the agency, on the back of a Big Idea.

The Big Idea is a key concept central to The Ogilvy Era. It's the "wow" factor agencies would pitch client brands. And with reason. In The Ogilvy Era, a good Big Idea could define or relaunch a brand. Pepsi was one of the first proponents of Big Idea advertising. When Pepsi wanted to create a strong message for its brand in the 1950s and 1960s it hired the agency BBDO to craft the "Pepsi Generation" advertising campaign.

A young blonde model's smile flashes a set of perfectly formed white teeth against the backdrop of a healthy California tan. It's monochrome, grainy film but you instantly feel the energy, warmth and color. She lifts her head back and swigs the soda.

"It's the official drink for everyone with a thirst for life."

Pepsi's Big Idea was a story of active fun, the blue skies of the Pacific and living for the moment. Before the Second World War, the target demographic was simply "children". But, in their own minds, teens were too worldly to be children and too carefree to be adults yet media rarely recognized their story. When Pepsi joined the dots, they helped shape a generation.

"This is the liveliest, most energetic time ever..." announces the voiceover, "with the most active generation living it."

It's a campaign that defined Pepsi and its brand for the best part of 50 years. And it served as a model for all marketers that followed.

The Big Idea is simple: get customers talking about your product by creating clever, fun or inspiring advertising. The more the advertising is of each of these, the more expensive it is, the more money the agency makes, the more likely it is to win awards. Tell 'em you're cool, tell 'em in a big way, tell 'em everyday. From the Pepsi Generation to Tony the Tiger, this is how we've been marketing since the 1950s.

Big Ideas made and broke brands because, back in The Ogilvy Era, advertising worked. Advertising gave us conversation. Foote Cone and Belding (now FCB) took claymation anthropomorphized grapes, set to Marvin Gaye's "Heard it through the Grapevine" and launched Californian Raisins, providing us with one of the most memorable ad campaigns of the era.

Think, for example, about how important campaigns like these were in defining their client companies:

- A Diamond is Forever: De Beers

- Is She Isn't She? Clairol
- Tony the Tiger: Kellogg's
- The American Dream: Fannie Mae
- The Pepsi Generation: Pepsi

If Twitter existed in 1989, the most popular trending buzzwords would have been #Madonna #MTV and #Pepsi. Pepsi paid Madonna $25 million to feature in a Pepsi Generation commercial aired once on MTV. In lunch halls, on campuses and in malls we talked about last night's commercial. "Did you see it?" became the hottest topic of the day.

Spending $25 million on an ad reassured the viewers that this brand had a lot of money because people just like them were buying their sodas. Big Ideas were just one great big testimonial. And brands were willing to pay that kind of money because Big Ideas worked. People watched TV, people talked about TV, people trusted TV. The whole advertising model was built in an era when customer trust and attention were abundant; that simply isn't true anymore.

But, Pepsi continues to wheel out the dancing bear, Beyoncé, for her new song "Grown Woman" as part of its latest campaign designed to target women. Brand managers forget that 1989 was nearly 30 years ago. As we've seen with Nokia and Microsoft, it's easier to do what you've always done, even if it doesn't work. No one gets fired for making an ad that doesn't work because it's play it safe. Who is going to be brave and do it differently?

BRAND IN THE CONNECTION ECONOMY

People don't wake up thinking about brands anymore. Young people aren't listening to Beyoncé like they used to listen to Madonna. Young people have choice. What counts now are the brands that young people can connect with, brands that present a face just like their own. Tyler isn't the Pepsi Generation. There are 1000s, no millions, of kids out there who grow up in fear of the improbable beauty and bodies of icons like Beyoncé. These are the same icons that peer out at them from the front pages of beauty magazines designed to make them feel ugly.

In the Connection Economy, we still identify with the people we trust. It's just that now, we don't trust the images on the silver screen, rather the people who look and feel just like ourselves. Advertising is less effective than word of mouth because we increasingly trust people we know, not people we know of.

PEOPLE: RECRUIT FANS, NOT EXPERIENCE

If you want to do like Monster, you have to be like Monster. Focus on being the story, not telling it. That means getting the right people on board.

Advertising people are trained to think in a certain way. Their experience and skill-sets are based on a model that worked in The Ogilvy Era. The most valuable people in this group are the ones that adapt to change, not necessarily the ones with the most experience. They see change coming. They know the Big Idea doesn't work anymore.

Being like Monster means starting the brand process day 1 in your recruitment. Focus on populating your team with people who "get it" rather than those who have extensive experience in marketing. As highlighted in this book, world class brands build teams around people outside the category, people with influential Ecosystems and people who are Fans of the brand. Nowhere do these brands build their teams around grizzled ad agency veterans.

CULTURE: LEARN TO SAY 'NO'

Monster made a concerted, conscious effort not to use advertising to build its brand. The key element here in the success story lies in the fact that *not advertising* was a conscious effort. Unless you declare your intention *not* to do something, chances are that people will gravitate towards what's commonly practiced.

But brand leadership means accepting you have to broach the uncomfortable subjects, like doing differently. Monster always faced external pressure from partners, particularly when entering new markets, to resort to advertising. It requires a certain type of courage and vision to say "no".

Behind Monster's strong brand leadership also lies an appetite to ask the difficult questions. Such as, why don't ad agencies advertise?

There is an old saying, "don't buy from the cobbler whose children have no shoes." The logic is that the cobbler may be able to make good shoes but if he doesn't even clothe his own children, what kind of a man is he?

Event companies throw their own events, website designers create their own websites and PR companies tout their own services. Why not ad agencies?

There are a number of reasons given why this apparent incongruence exists, ranging from the credible "they get their business from referral" or "their awards are their advertising" to the weak, "they are not very good at telling their own story."

Whatever the answer, we're left with an elephant in the room: ad agencies use different methods than the ones they sell to their clients. Whether referral or awards, most agencies get their business through word of mouth. So, why shouldn't their clients? Monster's success proves what Paid Media agencies knew all along: Earned Media is the most effective marketing of all.

The Yellow Brick Road is the whole charade of the Ogilvy Era model. The Yellow Brick Road always leads to the Emerald City. Everything about The Ogilvy Era is also geared to reinforce the advertising process:

- choice of metrics like "awareness", "brand equity" or "top of mind" to measure brand success
- award ceremonies
- the pitch process

If you want to do different, you not only have to *think* different about what brand is, you also have to *do* different. You have to avoid the charade of The Ogilvy Era if you want to avoid being dragged down The Yellow Brick Road.

Ogilvy Era agencies will always win out in the pitch process because that's what they do. Traditional advertising campaigns will always beat offline events or social media strategies because the metrics are geared in their favor. And, none of the brands in this book will ever win an award at Cannes because Cannes celebrates creativity, not marketing effectiveness.

If you're going to work with an agency, find one that is geared to a long term relationship, that isn't predetermined by the campaign model and isn't all about "wow" in the pitch process.

METRICS: YOU CAN'T BUILD A BRAND IN 30 DAYS

Metrics are the pivot point for the whole marketing industry. He who controls them, controls marketing. That's why advertising won't give up traditional Metrics. They'll insist on clients using these Metrics because it creates its own reliance on Big Idea advertising. After all, there is no more effective way of creating awareness than a big, expensive ad campaign. It's what we call agencies marking their own homework.

Cosmetic brand Dove released one of the most talked-about viral video campaigns in 2013, a campaign that invited "actors" to talk about sensitive issues such as beauty. Despite its immediate success, the campaign failed to generate sustainable interest. Measurable conversations about the Dove brand tracked on social media spiked in the first 7 days but then faded out to near zero after 30. That works in the world of ad agencies because by next month, everybody's moved on to the next big thing or the agency is already pitching the follow-up.

As long as we continue to focus on the short term impact of Paid Media alone we will never fully comprehend its true cost. What is the ROI on a campaign that disappears off the radar after 30 days?

Monster took 5 years to reach mainstream recognition in the US. That was 5 years they existed off the radar, unknown but to a few hardcore Motocross or drift fans. Could a brand grow in that environment if it needed results within 30 days? Probably not. But then, great brands aren't built in 30 days. Most people don't know that Zappos is over 15 years old, Apple took 20 years to deliver on its vision of building a brand around young customers, Starbucks is nearly 50 years old and GoPro is two years older than Facebook.

In 2014, Coca Cola bought a 16.7% stake in Monster for $2.15bn. No longer could big soda sit back and try to throw money at the market to keep the competition out. But as much as they appear fast paced and aggressive, brands like Monster know slow and steady wins the race. One Fan at a time. When Coca Cola bought in, big soda raised a white flag to winning in the youth space against authentic energy drinks brands that follow the new rules of marketing, not the old way. If we want to grow a brand with heart, we need to measure the effectiveness of our marketing over the long term, not just in windows convenient for the advertising agencies, stock markets and bosses only focused on next quarter.

CAN MONSTER CONTINUE TO BUILD A BRAND WORTH TALKING ABOUT?

Calling Monster's fortunes is tough. The soda industry changes so fast and long term dominance is very difficult to maintain without access to global distribution networks. Monster's recent tie up with Coke highlights the fact that even the best challenger brands can't do it all by themselves.

While Monster is significantly bigger than pioneer brand Jones Soda, it will face similar challenges:

- *Much of the success of the brand comes from long term investment in projects that don't have any obvious, short term benefit. In these conditions, it's easy for management who come into the brand from the outside, with little understanding of the brand's culture and scene, to push to cut these projects in favor of quick wins.*
- You also have to remember that Monster is a brand competing for customer mindshare with Coke and Red Bull. That's no easy task.

On the upside, there are many markets (such as Indonesia) where you can't buy Monster (yet) but teenagers are wearing the t-shirts and putting stickers on their bikes. In this context, the tie up with Coke makes sense.

Then there's the Monster alumni. It's always the mark of a strong brand that those who leave the company end up wanting to work with the company long term. The extreme sports and marketing industries have a growing number of ex-Monster people who help expand the brand's influence long term.

CHAPTER 8. SOUTHWEST AIRLINES: BRAND HAPPENS

❧❧❧❧❧

Southwest Airlines CEO - Gary Kelly as his alter ego Gene Simmons

DON'T FLY BRITISH AIRWAYS (AND OTHER BRAND STORIES)

"Don't fly with British Airways. They can't keep track of your luggage."

It's not an unusual gripe to hear among fellow passengers. But what made this particular tweet noteworthy was that the customer, Hasan Syed, spent $1000 promoting it on Twitter. The tweet was pushed out not only to 500 followers but to an extra 50,000 subscribers over the course of a week.

If you're going to create a brand in the Connection Economy, better make sure it's not one that pisses customers off. We all have gripes from time to time with companies, but what would compel a customer to actually spend so much money amplifying that gripe?

British Airways earned Syed's vitriol by losing his father's luggage for two days the weekend after a flight from Chicago to Paris. This mishap forced him to remain in Paris an extra night and cancel a trip to Dusseldorf, Germany. After calls to the airline's customer service department got them nowhere, Syed's father asked him to call the airline out online.

It's a brand and PR manager's worst nightmare: a customer complaint going viral, picked up by the mainstream media and ultimately ending up as a social media case study to stalk them for eternity. Sure, some airlines are better than others, but the fact remains that none are perfect: all airlines lose baggage all the time.

But, the key factor is this line in the story: "After calls to the airline's customer service department got them nowhere..."

Customers will forgive a brand for inconsistencies, for not being the cheapest or the coolest in the market, but they'll never forgive a brand that makes them feel bad.

Time to hit the NUKE button.

British Airways (BA) recently spent millions upgrading their brand for the 21st century, seeking out their creative agency's "Big Idea" to re-energize tired expectations. It started with the memos being sent by management to the workers...

"We have a light touch with words. We are polite. And finally, we have the same helpful, friendly personality whenever we communicate. We don't become bossy and distant in signs, put on a layer of management jargon when we speak to each other internally... We sound like British Airways, always."...said the British Airways brand template for the 21st century.

The document concludes with the statement: "We're moving our brand language forward".

The centerpiece of their 2012 relaunch with agency BBH was a nostalgic 90 second TV spot that paid tribute to early aviators and pilots who followed them. The campaign tried to evoke a sense of pride, of identity and unswerving devotion to the field of aviation. It coincided with the top-billing sponsorship of the London Olympics and local athletes like gold medalist heptathlete Jessica Ennis, supported by PR stunts and "experiential pop ups."

When companies struggle, it's not uncommon to press the "makeover" button. Agencies often sell the idea of a brand makeover as the magic wand that will cure all ills: a new logo, a fresh outlook and a revived spirit. BA has undergone several makeovers (face lifts?) in recent years:

"Upgrade to British Airways", "The World's Best Airline", "We'll Take More Care of You" and "Fly the Flag" are all slogans conceived by BA's creative agency blue sky thinkers over the years.

So why is it that despite these makeovers and the large sums spent with agencies, BA continues to annoy customers?

HOW CUSTOMERS EXPERIENCE BRANDS TODAY

Let's start by looking at what exactly defines a brand in everyday interaction. Consider the following story, in which a passenger experiences both the Southwest and Delta brand and then documents his journey.

The important part of this story is how the customer *experiences* the brand. It's completely subjective. As Jeff Bezos said earlier, your brand is what "people say about it..." Whether you agree or disagree with their interpretation, for that customer at least, their experience is 100% accurate.

Ken Krogue from Forbes flew two domestic flights with different airlines. The first flight was with Delta, a company known for the same failings as BA. The second was with Southwest Airlines, a younger upstart.

THE DELTA EXPERIENCE

Krogue's outbound flight was typical of a Delta experience. As a customer, he was a problem to the flight attendant trying to do her job. He got in the way.

"The lady on Delta got irritated at me because I had headphones on as we were taking off... she came back a little later and reminded me again because she noticed that the red light on my noise reducing headphones was still on, even though I had taken them off my ears and they were hanging loosely around my neck and my iPod was completely off as requested. She didn't seem happy to be there...At all."

Whether Krogue was right to complain about Delta is of no consequence. What matters is that he complained and now we all know about it. What matters is whether you side with Krogue or Delta. Based on your own experience, you might agree saying, "that's typical of a Delta flight."

"Halfway through the flight another Delta attendant came through pushing a cart and inquired about my beverage of choice. I asked for water. She handed me my water and a blue metallic bag of pretzels. I asked, 'Don't you have those awesome Delta cookies?' She said, 'Sorry, they didn't give us any on this flight.' "

Krogue's report is full of what many would call trivial incidents that could be perceived either way. Under a more positive light, the cookie incident could so easily have been a glowing homage to Delta's customer service.

"'Sorry', she said apologetically, 'they didn't give us any on this flight.' Full marks for trying though."

But that's not how Krogue told it and that's what counts. Krogue is right every time because he *owns* the experience.

THE SOUTHWEST AIRLINES EXPERIENCE

The pilot can't control the weather. The flight attendants can't control the baggage, gate catering arrangements or the drunk businessmen two rows back. And that's how every Delta and Southwest flight will be.

The difference is whether we choose to give those characters the benefit of the doubt.

"*Right after take off*," Krogue reports on the Southwest flight, "my Southwest flight attendant *came by quickly*, took my order for water. I was expecting peanuts. She came back in *short order* with a *full tray* of different beverages. She gave me my water and a yellow metallic bag of 'lightly salted peanuts' and a red bag of pretzels. Cool a bonus!"

Note the *emphasis* (mine) to show how customers *subjectively* interpret more or less the same experience based on whether they identify with the characters or not. Krogue identified with the SW attendant more than he did with the Delta one because the SW crew work within a culture that makes them more human. Rather than tie them down with BA-style brand diktats, SW people are given the freedom to behave naturally. We like humans. We dislike corporate robots.

"A jovial flight attendant on Southwest dedicated the flight to his in-laws and mentioned how grateful he was for them. A pilot came on and asked if there was anyone on the flight with an extra Valentines card for them in the cockpit. The flight attendant was young, smiling. The pilot was funny, but not over the top."

We identify with these characters. They are real, human and, unlike British Airways, forgivable.

PEOPLE: FOCUS ON WHAT'S IMPORTANT, NOT WHAT'S IN THE JOB DESCRIPTION

Job descriptions are what it says on the paper. It's what we do, what's expected of us and what we're measured against.

We all have job descriptions for legal reasons, even in flat management structures. But, job descriptions only become important when metrics are dysfunctional, demotivating or impossible.

Southwest pilots are famous for mucking in with the baggage handlers to get the cargo on board if the plane is running behind schedule. That creates a powerful brand experience for all passengers. We are more likely to forgive them for running late because we see them as human beings just like us.

Part of Southwest's ability to get people to do what's *needed* rather than do what's *written* in their job descriptions is their conscious decision to avoid "recruiting talent". Instead, preference when hiring is given to new people who will be able to integrate smoothly with other members on a team. There is a deliberate attempt to find people with the right attitudes first, and then provide them with the skills and experience they will need to excel. You'll find they don't necessarily hire for experience. They hire for ability with people. Someone with 10 years as an engineer may be less favored than a teacher with 10 years' experience. This may be an extreme example, but it shows experience in the domain is less important than experience with people.

Teachers, waiters and cops may be better *people*-people but they also have a key advantage over veterans: expectations. The point is that recruiting people from outside traditional circles helps break up the status quo, reduces reliance on old ways and helps release the stranglehold external agencies may have on the company.

"We would rather take an eager, hungry, customer-oriented mind and mold it to what works well at Southwest," said Sherry Phelps, an HR executive at Southwest with 33 years' experience, "than try to change the habits of someone who's come up through an organization that views life differently."

We hear a lot these days of questions like, "how can we engage our customers?" but companies look in all the wrong places for the answer.

Your answer lies here, in your own people. In its annual "American Workplace Survey", pollsters Gallup revealed the true state of employee engagement. Or maybe that should read *disengagement* because according to their findings, "70% of American workers are 'not engaged' or 'actively disengaged' and are emotionally disconnected from their workplaces and less likely to be productive."

Gallup's data showed:

- 30% of employees were Engaged
- 52% of employees were Disengaged
- 18% were Actively Disengaged

Gallup estimated that these actively disengaged employees cost the US between $450 and $550 billion each year in lost productivity. That's just the US. Globally, we're talking trillions of dollars. Disengaged employees were more likely to steal from their companies, negatively influence their coworkers, miss workdays, and drive customers away.

Think about how disengaged employees also shape your brand and how customers experience that brand. One grumpy flight attendant. One pilot on a "go slow" due to a union dispute. One ground staff who digs her heels in when a customer misses a flight and is unable to get home tonight. All of these daily interactions supersede any brand story created by the agency.

Imagine you had Zappos employees or Apple Genius crew running the airline. You wouldn't need to spend millions on advertising. Whether you're an airline or a bank, your people make all the difference. Get the people right and brand will fall into place.

CULTURE: LEAD BY EXAMPLE

Marketers often have difficulty pinning down the secret of brands like Apple, Virgin or Southwest Airlines. On the face of it, their brand templates are easily mimicked by others but something at the heart of the brand keeps turning out experiences that are exceptional rather than the norm.

The key is *leadership*. The people at the top. Everyone leads by example and the example that leaders need to set in the Connection Economy is that of removing the fear. Fear kills more dreams than failure ever will. When your people are fearful of making mistakes, they follow the rules. When people follow the rules, you end up with robots and customers hate robots.

You can encourage people to behave naturally a number of ways:

- Remove fear and unnecessary bureaucracy
- Trust in the people to do the right thing
- Set the example from the top that failure is okay

Southwest Airlines CEO Gary Kelly is well known for his open and flamboyant attitude towards corporate communication. At the company's Halloween party he's dressed up as Edna Turnblad from the musical Hairspray, Dorothy from the Wizard of Oz and Gene Simmons from Kiss.

"As long as you don't mind being ridiculed all day," he said in an interview to the New York Times, "it's part of the routine."

If CEO Kelly is willing to come down from his ivory tower, then his people will too. Southwest is legendary for having pilots who are willing to help load luggage if that's what it takes to get away on time. What other airline does this? A willingness to do what's important rather than what's in the rulebook is indicative of the flexible job boundaries which exist throughout the entire company, where anyone is willing to pitch in wherever required.

By contrast, BA execs rarely come out of their ivory tower. BA is a company plagued by industrial disputes between management and employees. It loses around $250m a year due to industrial action, last year alone seeing 22 days lost to walkouts. It's a "them and us" spat that often spills out into the press. BA's CEO Willie Walsh (nicknamed "Slasher") is often quoted as saying management will not yield to union demands. He was quoted by the Irish Prime Minister Bertie Ahern as being of "a time when management wanted to steal the assets for themselves through a management buy out, shafting staff interests." Not only is it a brand of yesteryear, it feels like we're stuck in the 80s all over again.

Willie Walsh sets the tone of an organization that holds its employees in contempt. Contempt is built on distrust and mistrust leads to control.

BA is all about top-down management of the brand:

- Consistency
- Centralization
- Control

These aren't 3 words we picked but ones that jumped out from their brand identity guide by creatives Schawk, an agency that offers to "*produce* and *protect* your brand". But, you can't produce and protect a brand in the Connection Economy. **Dialog is out there whether you like it or not.**

A thousand conversations are happening right now:

- The way your cabin crew greets your customers when they board the plane.
- The enthusiasm your field sales staff carry to the community event.
- The conversation between your product manager and the enthusiast about her latest project at the convention.

Your brand becomes the aggregate of each of these conversations, transmitted by Facebook, Instagram, Pinterest, YouTube and Twitter from the customer to 100 other people.

Perhaps it's uncomfortable for BA execs to look inside the company for the answer: too much history, too many no-go areas, too many vested interests. But, that's exactly what they need to do. Painting the words "to fly, to serve" on the tail fins of BA's fleet makes little difference when your average flight attendant turns up to work harassed by the work environment and insecure of her future.

You can't control the brand anymore. Brand happens. You can't manage it or create it. You can only curate the best of your own people.

METRICS: MEASURE WHAT REALLY MATTERS

In the Connection Economy, we need to measure what matters.

BA's own measures are vanity metrics. Their own measure of success? A 19% increase (to 54%) of awareness of BA's sponsorship of the Olympic Games. With much pride, BA's own brand spokesperson announced they had surpassed Adidas and Visa. Awareness of an ad campaign is no measure of success in The Connection Economy when the rubber hits the road. All bets are off.

What matters is what happens *right now:* the words your flight attendant says, the way your call center staff greets the caller and the smile on the face of your retail employee. Everything else is detail.

So, if we want to create an exceptional brand, we need to give those involved in creating the experience at the Frontline metrics that can make a difference, not metrics which are already decided by an outside force and beyond their ability to change.

Southwest airlines leads its category on both brand recommendation and sales growth. The brand has a Net Promoter Score of +55% (a measure of how much customers would recommend the brand to a friend). Compare that with the nearest rivals Continental at 32% and Delta at 10%.

Despite little money spent on advertising, Southwest has a 5 year sales growth of 12% per annum, ahead of the nearest rival Continental at 4% and followed by Delta at just 1.5%. If you want to grow through recommendation you need to measure it, you need to share that data with your people and you need to measure them according to their ability to contribute to a better experience.

CAN SOUTHWEST AIRLINES CONTINUE TO BUILD A BRAND WORTH TALKING ABOUT?

Southwest continues to be the brand people want to talk about. Sure, there are videos and blog posts about what Southwest gets wrong, but plenty more about what it gets right. Here's why, however, we think that situation may change long term:

- *Aviation isn't a clear cut industry. There are so many variables beyond the control of a single brand. Obvious factors include security, airports and fuel costs. But, on top of that you also have government regulation. Governments will always favor incumbent carriers, and grant them privileges not afforded to airlines like Southwest. Challenger brands like Southwest have adapted to this unfair environment but it doesn't mean that future changes can't ground their model.*

- Extending the point above, it's quite possible a new entrant unfairly subsidized by a foreign government, or a low cost carrier can erode Southwest's market share. While we don't think that will stop people talking about Southwest per se, it may exert pressure at their weakest point and commit the brand to some form of reactive short-term measure like a price war that may eventually unravel the brand.

CHAPTER 9. WAHOO'S FISH TACOS: BUILD A BRAND ON ITS ECOSYSTEM

১৯৯৯১৯

Wahoo's Fish Tacos CEO - Wing Lam

HOW WING GOT HIS START

Wahoo's Fish Tacos, founded by Wing Lam, is based in California.

It's the quintessential immigrant boy come good story with a twist. Where most immigrants are attracted to the startup scene of The Valley or the financial sector of San Francisco, Wing Lam wanted to do things differently.

Wing grew up in a multicultural environment. Born and raised in Sao Paulo's Chinatown, his father uprooted their family and moved to California in the mid-70s. It's there he and his three brothers discovered their love of surfing.

As the brothers got older, their surfing trips took them south of the border to Tijuana where they experienced authentic tacos served up on the beachfront with scraps from the fishermen's daily catch.

"They couldn't do anything with the accidental catches, like if they get a shark in with the tuna, or some other fish they couldn't sell," Wing said. "They'd call it a byproduct and give it to local vendors. You couldn't make filet of shark, because nobody would buy it, at least not back then. So they'd cut it in strips, deep fry it, and sell it in a fish taco. They were delicious."

By the late 80s, Wing was juggling with career options. His father was in the restaurant business. His older brother was making a career for himself in finance. But, deep down, Wing just wanted to surf.

What if he could mix up those interests and set up a restaurant that allowed him to make money and surf at the same time? That way he could stay connected with the people and the scene.

"I thought I'd have one little taco stand in Costa Mesa and be able to surf all the time," he said, his logic being that Costa Mesa was but a stone's throw from some of the best breaks on the West Coast. "I still get to surf"

"The original idea was to create a restaurant that was to the surf industry what the Hard Rock Café was to music. We had grown up surfing and we knew what surfers liked. In the '80s, surfers from California would drive down to Mexico to surf and we'd all eat fish tacos; we all talked about how great they were. We also had a feel for the sort of mellow, chill atmosphere that would appeal to surfers."

Lam brought his unique combination of Mexican, Brazilian and Asian influences to the surfers of California. And, while there are many taco and fusion options on the market, what makes Wahoos unique is its connection with the surfing Ecosystem.

"I had this idea that I wanted to be where the surfers are. You can't be in Riverside to do that. So we opened our first store in Costa Mesa where all the big surf companies in the world have their U.S. operations. If I cater to them, eventually they will come. So if the concept is that it's a restaurant for surfers, you can decorate the restaurant to reflect that."

Being based in Costa Mesa meant Lam's first taco joint was on the doorstep of the head offices of brands like Billabong and Quiksilver. Surfers and their execs would drop in after catching the morning swell or at lunch. Eating a Taco at Wahoo's is like eating at a surf shop. Surfers would say, "That's a place that I would like to eat because I'm welcome. That feels like home."

"I remember the first summer we were open, which was the summer of '89, I had guys like Tom Curren, Mark Occhilupo, Martin Potter – surfers who were world champions," he recalls, "coming in for lunch with their sponsors."

By putting the surf Ecosystem at the heart of the brand, Wahoo's connection to the scene helped fuel brand success. Wing Lam doesn't hang out with surfers because he knows word of mouth spreads fast in their scene. He hangs out with surfers because he's one of them. But it doesn't just end with setting up on the doorstep of the scene you want to be part of. It also requires a lot of hustle.

Every other brand is trying to break into the surf scene. Street wear, watches, auto and even health insurance. They're all there with their booths at surf shows. They're there when they want to tell you about their brand or sell you something. But, they're never there when it comes to supporting the scene. And that's what makes Wahoo's both different and a brand with an authentic heart. A big part of Wing's success is getting out there and being seen, being active and giving back generously to the scene. Whenever there's an event, Wing is there in his food truck, often giving out free food.

When he's not surfing, he's skating. When the opportunity came up to cater for a Tony Hawk event because other retailers couldn't meet the terms, Wing jumped at the chance. He's still out there making tacos at events, connected with the community on authentic terms. Lam also plays an active role in surf nonprofits like the Surfrider Foundation, dedicated to protecting the coastline. He caters for their events for free and receives no compensation for the time he gives. He pays to attend board meetings out of his own pocket.

He also helps other companies in Southern California who are making products for his tribe. For example, he created an event for a new rock climbing gym in Costa Mesa. Of course, Wing supplied the free food. If these companies grow, they grow together. Wing markets the company through events, surfing contests, skateboard contests, snowboard exhibitions and extreme sports events such as the X-Games—which has since become a highly popular annual extreme sports showcase. He says promos take "a lot of time and effort," but the company did them for one reason: money. "When you don't have a lot of money, the best way to sample is through events," he said. "You rely on other people."

"I love spending time in my little taco truck and making tacos at events," he says. "I probably do it two or three times a week. People ask, 'Don't you have anything better to do?' But the satisfaction of serving someone something really good is really great. It's a total passion for me."

It's a gesture that many would frown at: why cheapen your product by giving it away for free? But, Wing is convinced if people taste his food, they will want it on a regular basis. And further to that, surfers look after their own.

It was the surf companies and their people that helped get the original Wahoo's off the ground. As Wing didn't have any money to invest in marketing, he turned to the Ecosystem and they helped him out, providing furniture and decorations for the Costa Mesa store.

As Lam says, "They made it their own."

Wahoo's is growing.

Today, the company has revenues in excess of $100 million with stores opening throughout the States. But it's not a rapid outburst of stores but a controlled organic process, meeting new markets where the demand pulls it.

Surfers from Chicago come down to California during their breaks, eat at Wahoos and then want to remember those times when they are back in the gray north dreaming about their next trip.

"It somehow appeals," said Carol Schauer, director of operations for Wahoo's of Colorado, which now operates 11 units in the state. "Whether or not you're in California, there's an attraction to the community of surfing, snowboarding, those types of activities."

FIND YOUR ECOSYSTEM

"For millions of years, human beings have been part of one tribe or another. A group needs only two things to be a tribe: a shared interest and a way to communicate." - Seth Godin.

Find the Ecosystem where your brand can grow. Find your tribe, your home, the place where you belong. Grow your brand there. Respect the dynamics and relationships and the Ecosystem will look after you long term.

Ecosystems are natural, authentic networks based on real world scenes. Each Ecosystem has its own protocol, from the language used to the clothes worn. These networks possess a code often hidden to the outsider that reinforces social dynamics like who's "in", who's "out" and who the key influencers are.

It's easy to see how an energy drink brand can partner with dirt bikers, BMXers or freedivers. But, what about a bank?

Ecosystems could be a scene like punk rock or snowboarding. Equally, they could be the sphere of influence that any of your team has, from your marketing intern to your CEO. An Ecosystem could be a non-physical concept, like an idea or a Pain Point as discussed in the next section.

Because so much of the early success in engaging Ecosystems came from action sports, it can appear that Ecosystems = Action Sports, but that's not the case. Any network of people can be an Ecosystem. A network of young startup entrepreneurs is an Ecosystem that a bank can tap into; a network of world travelers is one for an insurance company; shoppers disenchanted with customer service is prime for an online retailer.

The point is find the Ecosystem that matches your own brand's heart. You can't fake it. If you're a bank manager and you don't surf or your bank isn't a bank for surfers, don't buy your way into the surf scene. Rather, look at the Ecosystems where you do belong, where you're connected already.

PEOPLE: ECOSYSTEMS START WITH YOUR OWN PEOPLE

It's tempting to go out there looking for an Ecosystem or to look to your agency to shop around for one, but it needs to be authentic, based on your real world relationships.

If your marketing intern starts talking about your latest products with his tribe, they'll find out about it in a quicker and more trusted way then waiting for the ad campaign to come round. We've always had Ecosystems. But, what's changed now is that we have the technology for Ecosystems to easily share information. In the Connection Economy, your whole marketing team now becomes your payroll, plus their respective Ecosystems.

By understanding your natural connections, marketing becomes less about buying media and more about winning over your own people. If you can create a positive culture and an empowered, happy, workforce, your company brand message flows naturally through all the Ecosystems connected to your company by virtue of your staff's own personal networks.

If you want to get a better understanding of what Ecosystems you are part of, ask your staff to map their own ones out. By mapping Ecosystems you get a better idea of how and to which natural networks you are already connected to, without resorting to traditional marketing. Perhaps someone knows a magazine editor, an athlete, a DJ, a designer and so on?

Everybody has one – from the CEO to your frontline staff to the customer. Everybody is connected with other people and within that network they have some degree of influence. You influence people at work. You are influenced by your surfing buddies. Your boss is influenced by an old friend from college. Your spouse influences friends at her yoga class.

A telecom brand could find that its own people are connected to magazine editors, writers and photographers within a scene it's already trying to reach through expensive top-down marketing.

In building the brand, every employee now has a role to play.

When you start seeing your Ecosystem as a vital part of your brand marketing strategy, you also see how important recruitment becomes in shaping your brand.

Start measuring recruits based on their influence within the Ecosystem:

- Who are they connected to?
- Who do they have access to?
- What events, societies, networks and clubs do they belong to?
- What are their hobbies, interests and passions?

In traditional brand setups, the VP recruits marketers with strong agency backgrounds. But often these career marketers don't have the most effective Ecosystems to leverage for the brand. Today, an ex-journalist, athlete or DJ could be a far more effective hire than an ex-agency professional.

Brands like Monster Energy place emphasis on recruiting people from the scenes they wanted to penetrate. Southwest airlines favors teachers, firefighters and people with retail experience over cabin crew from rival airlines. Insurance companies targeting the travel sector should recruit travel bloggers.

Build your team around people who have a track record of influencing others. They understand how to create influence within these networks; they talk the language, understand the protocols and have instant respect. You can't buy this kind of authenticity.

CULTURE: FIND THE SHARED EMOTION

Ecosystems are often less about physical scenes and more about shared emotions.

Ecosystems are often built on a mutual *pain point.* What counts is your ability to understand the pain. Surfing is built on a desire to escape the mediocrity of modern life and taste freedom on the swell. Entrepreneurs want a better life out of the corporate cubicle. Online shoppers want service from people they can trust, who treat them like they want their business.

In a RIAA & Harris Interactive poll of online music customers, they found that 77% of people surveyed said, "not having a credit card" was one of the top 5 barriers to legal music downloads. Other complaints included "file not compatible with devices" (63%) and can't share song files (58%). Only 17% said "slow speed" represented a barrier to usage. What unites a future music Ecosystem may be less about an interest in a specific genre but a problem they collectively face.

Clearly, pain points exist and they open a market opportunity for brands associated with the Ecosystem to provide a solution.

Pure Digital's Flip (the handheld video camera) was built on the premise that youth wanted a cheap, light handheld that had enough functionality to shoot video but nothing more. Focus group research found that youth wanted "Bluetooth", "connectivity", "cheaper" and so on. It's only when Pure Digital gave the Flips to young people for a month to play with the device that they discovered what was later to become the device's defining feature. Youth didn't carry cables so they were inevitably stuck with all this content on their devices which eventually rendered them useless.

Designers took this insight back to the drawing board and remodeled the device by adding a simple pop-out USB adapter. Many competitor devices had these simple add ons today, but at the time (2006) the Flip was nothing short of revolutionary.

PD discovered a *pain point* it couldn't find in the development process through traditional market research. Getting out there and partnering with the Ecosystem was key to an insight that gave them a market lead.

Despite generating over $600m in sales long before GoPros ever hit the market, PD's acquirer Cisco pulled the plug on the project. Cisco could be sitting on the next GoPro today but it isn't. Cisco didn't retain their connection with the Ecosystem and were unable to see beyond the product-focused, category-based benchmarks that reduced the Flip to a like-for-like comparison with the nearest rivals.

Zappos isn't action sports or punk music, but an Ecosystem of people connected through a feeling, in particular people dissatisfied with something. It's as powerful a relationship as one connected through a tangible hobby or sport. In the Zappos example, you have people dissatisfied with customer service or retail shopping. They share a common feeling and that connects them as an Ecosystem. What it takes is a leader like Tony Hsieh to plant a flag for these people to rally around.

By asking the question "what's not exciting and painful about online shopping?", Zappos was able to identify the rallying points for the Ecosystem. In this case issues like returns, trust and shipping costs. It's these insights that led Hsieh to believe with conviction that providing outstanding customer service at any cost was core to growth. So by building a business around the shared emotion of the ecosystem, Zappos was able to use this existing network of influence as a powerful base for their brand.

These Ecosystems aren't obvious so it takes great brands like Wahoo's, Zappos or Pure Digital to create them.

As much as Ecosystems live and feel, they also have their own memories and legacies. They soon learn whether you are here to grow with them or here just to score a few points.

Each Ecosystem has rules to respect, goodwill and grudges. If you treat an Ecosystem badly, don't expect people in that network to come to your aid in future. If you don't know the code and the protocol, you're in the wrong Ecosystem. Your people should know instinctively based on their own experience and relationships. You shouldn't need to ask.

Every brand has to earn its place in the Ecosystem. You can't take shortcuts, you can't buy your way on to the top table; you have to plant seeds and grow your relationships organically. Sure, people will readily take your bag of money when you're knocking at the door of a scene trying to get in, but that won't help you build trust or attention over the long term. This is the mistake Sony made when trying to curate its PlayStation fan base.

Koushik Dutta is a revered programmer within Android circles. He's also a fan of PlayStation products. Sony put 2 and 2 together, reaching out to Dutta in the hope of luring him to work for them on a series of exciting product lines. Dutta refused, turning down a plum job, because of Sony's history; Sony famously prosecuted hacker George Hotz (GeoHot) for his PSP3 mods and Dutta felt that although he was fond of their products – he hated the company. Ecosystems have longer memories than the average brand manager.

METRICS: THINK LONG TERM WITH THE ECOSYSTEM

You have to go into an Ecosystem with a long term mindset. You can't expect results overnight. Relationships take time. Don't rush or sweat them. Winning over Ecosystems requires a long term approach of sitting back and letting the Ecosystem do what it does without interference. Be seen to be taking part and supporting the connections rather than getting in the way.

Ecosystems only yield dividends if you approach them long term and adopting the right, long term metrics is key. If you expect an Ecosystem to yield results next quarter, you'll be disappointed. Results take time.

In 2011, Converse opened a free recording studio called Rubber Tracks in Brooklyn to help new emerging artists gain access to resources they may not have been able to afford.

During its 80-year history, Converse sold 170 million pairs of the black canvas sneaker with white rubber sole – the Chuck Taylor All-Stars – in 144 countries. Yet, by 2001 the company had filed for bankruptcy only to be rescued by the unlikeliest of suitors – Nike – in 2003. Converse had a long tradition of market influence – here was a brand once worn by Larry Bird, Dr. J, Elvis Presley, Magic Johnson and Kurt Cobain because it stood for something and had built that brand story over the long term.

The underground punk rock scene bought into Converse because it also stood for the anti-establishment. Here was a basic shoe canvas that could be co-opted and recreated with a simple Sharpie permanent marker. The white canvas became a storyboard for expression for wannabe Kurt Cobains.

Red Bull did the same with its Music Academy, LEGO in supporting its AFOL community and Monster with its Army. Take a small % of the budget and ring fence it. Sell the case that this will take years to mature but ultimately it's going to help across the board when it does. Sometimes these projects can't be measured in terms of traditional metrics today but need to happen purely based on your feeling for the Ecosystem.

CAN WAHOO'S CONTINUE TO BUILD A BRAND WORTH TALKING ABOUT?

When it comes to building a brand worth talking about and Wahoo's, so far so good. Wahoo's has vocal fans and a community to build on. These assets don't go away overnight. Wahoo's continues to grow off the back of customers "pulling" it into new markets rather than aggressive expansion plans that may lead to overstretch.

Here a reasons why Wahoo's growth may stall long term:

- *Wahoo's' biggest challenge is remaining relevant in the fiercely competitive "fast casual dining" market. In this sector alone you have a new breed of dynamic brands like Chipotle Mexican Grill, In-N-Out Burger and Shake Shack who have already built vocal beachheads of Fans.*
- *You also have to consider the growing popularity of the food truck movement which is able to offer customers cheaper, more experimental fare without the overhead of a brick-and-mortar restaurant.*
- Starbucks and McDonald's are also outside competition. They all compete for customer time, wallet and, importantly, conversations. Starbucks will always remain a threat, especially if it decides to extend its menu into Wahoo's territory. McDonald's is more of an unknown. At time of writing, McDonald's is desperately trying to innovate its way out of a hole. There is a good chance McDonald's will end up back where it started after some "window dressing" to placate the public (like it did following the "Super Size Me" scandals) but there is also the possibility McDonald's could decide on some more wholesale reinvention and chase the fast casual market which would make it a direct competitor with Wahoo's.

CHAPTER 10. APPLE STORE: BUILDING A BRAND AT THE FRONTLINE

৶৶৶৶৶

Head of Apple Retail - Ron Johnson

THE APPLE STORE SUCCESS STORY

"In the city that never sleeps, neither does this store!"

Ron Johnson welcomes media, analysts and VIPs as the first to try out the new Apple store located on Fifth Avenue between 58th and 59th Streets, New York.

It's 6pm, May 19th. It's a Friday evening, an unusual time for a store opening but then Apple is throwing out the rule book. Customers don't seem to mind. A line snakes several times around the block. The first person in line according to a fan website is "Stormy Shippy, [who] arrived from Texas and took his place at 12:15 a.m." Excited and anxious, Apple Fans wait under umbrellas and a mini tarpaulin city sheltering their Macbooks. Some are here to win one of the many giveaways gifts, others just for the ride.

Apple's senior vice president of Retail, Johnson, explains that the new store will be open 24 hours a day and 365 days a year.

"We don't want a visitor [to New York City] to miss a chance to come to the Apple Store," and added, "this store will be open from today forever."

The store is a 32 foot glass cube that sits in the middle of the square leading down a spiral staircase and glass elevator into Apple's cavernous 10,000 square foot below-ground emporium. Some describe it as "beautiful." Today, it's one of the most photographed landmarks in New York. Combined with the store's iconic design, Johnson's statement is a signal of intent: Apple's future is here at the Frontline.

Looking at the numbers, you'd have to agree:

Apple Store growth:

- Today, 62% of Apple's US payroll works for its retail stores. What other tech brand could boast such commitment to stores?
- The number of Apple stores globally increased to 421 in 2013 from 380 in 2012. Revenue per store increased from $51 million per store in 2012 to $55 million in 2013.
- Apple stores recorded a per square foot sales figure of $6,050 in 2013 – two times the per square foot sales figure of Tiffany & Co. ($3,017). Electronic megastore Best Buy clocked in at $808 per square foot.
- Apple store visitors globally increased from 320 million in 2012 to 395 million in 2013. That's more than three times the number of annual visitors to Disney Parks globally (125 million) or the number of Super Bowl viewers (111.3 million).
- Apple Stores globally see on average 50,000 Genius Bar visits a day. That's the capacity of Yankee Stadium.

Apple Store and Brand Experience
- Apple Stores create loyalty and word of mouth through positive customer experience. Apple has ranked as the #1 smartphone brand in the J.D. Power and Associates Smartphone Satisfaction Study since 2009.
- Positive experience also increases Apple customer loyalty by 8.2% and the likelihood of recommendation by 8.4%. This resulted in additional revenues of $219 million over a one year period (2013).
- Apple customers who bought their smartphone in an Apple store are 5 times more likely to be loyal (i.e. buy a new iPhone when it's time to upgrade contract) than Apple customers who bought online via a mobile carrier like Verizon or AT&T.

HOW THE APPLE STORE WAS NOT JUST ABOUT THINKING DIFFERENTLY, BUT DOING DIFFERENTLY

Apple's Stores weren't always such a clear-cut business case. Apple took a big risk on their Frontline.

Firstly, there weren't many people trained for the job Apple was hiring for. Most IT retailers relied on big box sellers. While Apple has a whole army of passionate Genius employees today, before it launched the stores, Apple retail specialists were extremely rare. Johnson wasn't sure he could get the caliber of Frontline staff that could carry the Apple brand experience. As it turned out, there were plenty of young Apple enthusiasts who applied: 5,000 applied for the 300 jobs at the Fifth Avenue store.

Secondly, it was a departure from the norm. Before they launched their own store, Apple was reliant on others. As Ron Johnson explains it, the whole experience became hostage to the People, Culture and Metrics of other retailers who they had to distribute through. For too long they relied on undertrained and unmotivated Best Buy staff who cared little about the Apple experience and, even if they did, weren't the experience the brand was seeking. Back then, customers went to a technology store to acquire a product, and it was often an awful experience driven by a salesperson on commission whose main interest was in emptying your wallet.

By contrast, Apple Store associates are not on commission. They don't try to sell you anything. They have one job: to help you find the product that's right for you, even if it's not an Apple product. All those things create value beyond the transaction.

Thirdly, it requires investment. It's cheaper to outsource. Most companies do, whether it's a store, event management or a call center.

160

But, despite these 3 apparent risks, Apple prioritized the roll out of Apple stores. People often talk up Apple's products and design philosophy as key to their success but we believe this is once again reinforcing the mysticism of brand. Apple didn't design radical products, it designed a radical customer experience.

"You've got to start with the customer experience and work back toward the technology – not the other way around." – Steve Jobs.

Apple isn't so much an IT company today but a retail brand. Like Apple, you need to get away from a mindset that confines you to a set of paradigms. You don't have to create a retail presence, but you need a Frontline. Bank, insurance company or mobile phone manufacturer, you all can have a Frontline. It's here your brand lives and dies. When you aren't in control of the brand experience at the Frontline, your market is easily assailed by competition. The reverse is also true. With a strong Frontline presence, competition has a hard time getting a foothold in the market, regardless of the depth of resources they have to offer. Frontlines may cost money. It may be cheaper to outsource but it always costs you more in the long term.

HOW FRONTLINES DRIVE BUSINESS

In the Connection Economy, Frontlines count.

Frontlines create experiences that customers share. Think what happens after those 50,000 people visit the Apple Genius Bar. Frontlines create loyal Fans. Apple ranks #1 in terms of customer satisfaction and word of mouth in the mobile industry.

Every brand manager strives for these kindd of results, but not every brand manager cares to look inside the business for answers.

Think about customer loyalty again. All of the brands in this book are built on a beachhead of loyal Fans. But, what creates that loyalty? It doesn't start outside the business with an ad campaign or loyalty program. Loyalty isn't a product of discounts either. Try get one of those at an Apple store.

Take a look at the data on customer loyalty. Why do companies lose customers? According to a survey by the American Society for Quality, here's why:

- Customer dies: 1%
- Customer moves away: 3%
- Customer influenced by friends: 5%
- Customer lured away by competition: 9%
- Customer dissatisfied by product: 14%
- Customer turned away by attitude of indifference by provider: 68%

Look at that data again.

The attitude of your Frontline staff is nearly 8 times more important in maintaining customer loyalty than the strategies of your competitors. Marketers tend to think that customers switch because of better brands, better products, better offers elsewhere. This is rarely the case. Customers tend to stick around. They don't like change. Customers will pay more, settle for less because they are comfortable or familiar with a product or service.

They'll forgive you not having the coolest product, the cheapest product or the best offers in the market. But what they won't forgive is when you make them feel bad.

PEOPLE: FIND YOUR FRONTLINE

Many people talk about Apple's design philosophy and Jobs' leadership as key to the brand's success. While these have shaped the company's fortunes, nothing has been more important to the brand than the success of its retail stores.

Think about that for a minute. If you think Apple's success is about technology or design, that's what you're going to focus more on. If you think it's about people, you'll commit to a Frontline. The Frontline is the touch point between your customer and the company; the point at which they experience your brand first hand.

Example Frontlines:

- Call center
- Retail store
- Community
- Event
- Social project

Each has the ability to transform the brand experience for that one customer as either something positive or negative, way beyond the scope of what traditional marketing can do.

When you lose your Frontline, you also lose focus.

You decouple your brand from the market. Brands slide into irrelevance. Metrics become irrelevant. Companies adopt cultures of denial. People become driven by fear, insecure about their future or position in the company.

We've seen it with Nokia, Microsoft and BA. It happens to the best of companies. Kodak, for example, was perhaps one of the most innovative companies of the 20th century. But the Kodak story of success is also a familiar story of failure. Sometimes brands become so successful they become complacent; they feel they don't need to build a Frontline to stay relevant.

On March 26th, 2007, Eastman Kodak announced it was resigning from the "Council of Better Business Bureaus" after expulsion proceedings were issued by the Bureau. BBB is an industry standards body that aims to promote a "marketplace where businesses and consumers can trust one another." The Bureau helps its members reduce the distance between customer and employee by sharing best practices, member case study insights and offering training. Its motto is "Start with trust."

When the BBB warned Kodak of expulsion, it provided extensive documentation of how the brand became synonymous with customer dissatisfaction. Many were disgruntled with Kodak's customer service. Customers said cameras broke and they were charged for repairs even though failure was not the result of damage or abuse. Some say their cameras failed repeatedly even after numerous returns to the engineering department. Despite obvious public dissent with brand, product and service, Kodak continued to trumpet their successes. The irony wasn't how such an iconic American brand had lost the plot, it was (according to Kodak) the service meted out to the BBB itself.

When you create a company so hierarchical, so removed from the heart of the brand, you also create a culture of denial.

"If I said it was raining, nobody would argue with me, even if it was sunny outside" said ex-CEO Antonio Perez in an interview with BusinessWeek.

"We handled 99% of the complaints listed," claimed a Kodak spokesperson. "Ironically, we ultimately decided to resign our membership because we were extremely unhappy with the customer service we received from the local office of the BBB."

Like schoolyard politics, Kodak resigned from the BBB before the BBB ousted Kodak.

The origins of Kodak's failure aren't found in any specific strategy or decision but, rather, a detachment from the Frontline. Kodak was a company of disjointed interests and silos that weren't either motivated or encouraged to communicate with both each other and the customer.

When Kodak slid into bankruptcy, Kodak's Chief Blogger reported the "good news" from the Consumer Electronics Show (CES):

- "Kodak Hero Inkjet printers getting attention at CES - so many ways to print! - Google Cloud, smart phones!" she tweeted.
- Kodak's chief blogger, on the other hand, tried to whitewash the failure of her organization suggesting it was business as usual in her tweets. "FYI Kodak's not dead yet, guys. You can still buy their amazing film. #believeinfilm @kodakCB"
- "Customers can count on Kodak for business as usual. Same quality products & services that they have come to expect"
- "@alfredopalconit Kodak is not gone - it's a filing for reorganization through Chapter 11 process"

The sad aftermath of this story is that Kodak, a once iconic and pioneering brand, could be in the mobile business today. But it isn't. On January 2012, Kodak filed for Chapter 11 bankruptcy protection. However you want to spin it, Chapter 11 pretty much means the writing is on the wall.

Kodak failed only a month after Apple launched its 5th and biggest store in Manhattan, Apple Grand Central. Their fortunes could not be any further removed. Apple reported quarterly revenues of $46.33 billion and sales of 37 million iPhones (an increase of 127% on the same quarter the year before).

Ironically, like Apple, Kodak had some of the brightest brains in the business working on new products. But, unless those products are based on what's happening at the Frontline, it's all academic. In the Connection Economy, the Frontline becomes the moment of truth, where the marketing rubber hits the road. It's there that the nature of the company becomes an incontrovertible truth.

CULTURE:
SELL THE FRONTLINE INTERNALLY

The Frontline is traditionally the first part of a business to get outsourced.

Call centers, for example, are often seen as cost centers in so many COO eyes. It could easily be outsourced to Gurgaon for a fraction of its current operating costs. You could even charge customers a premium rate number to access it. Operatives trained in an irritating game of '20 questions' innocently tend to the inquiries of customers. Then there's "press 1 for sales". Few leave with a positive experience. Many hang up and turn to "call center rage", venting their frustration at an innocent trainee, or simply resign to acquiescence.

Costs fall in the short term but rise in the long term because customer service is also your best marketing strategy. Outsourcers lose customers and that costs a lot of money to recoup.

Take a look at Apple's rivals in the retail space:

"In recent years, both Best Buy and Sears have shuttered hundreds of physical stores, reducing the human interactions that help customers feel comfortable buying online. And so far, Best Buy's effort to embrace 'showrooming' by customers has been insufficient to counter its smaller retail footprint, as its revenue has steadily declined this year." - Fidelum Partners research, "What Zappos is Teaching Amazon About E-commerce Loyalty", 2014.

"Just a few years ago, Best Buy was hailed as one of the finest retailers in the world. It had vanquished its rival, Circuit City, and was likely selling more electronics per square foot than any other company. But by 2012 it was in tatters." - Michael Copeland, Wired headline, 2013.

When you change your view of what the Frontline is, you change its role at the heart of the brand.

"Imagine a friendly place that dispenses advice and is staffed by the smartest Mac person in town. He would be like a genius to the customer, because he knows so much." - Ron Johnson on the creation of the Genius Bar. An Apple Genius employee can make customers feel good, appease their fears and teach them something useful that they can take away and share with friends. By committing resources to the experience, Apple wants to make that experience friendly, trustworthy and useful. Ron Johnson changed Apple's view of what the Frontline was. Where rivals were replacing their Frontlines with cheap alternatives in India or outsourcing it to big box retailers, Apple did the opposite: it invested in its own people.

A key way to strengthen the role of the Frontline and place it at the Heart of the Brand is to change how your people view the organization. Consider, for example, the Pyramid: the traditional organizational structure. A few elite managers at the top controlling resources and information.

In the Connection Economy, brands need to turn that whole structure upside down, or "flipping the pyramid" as we call it. This is not a physical process but a mental one. Often you can achieve this by simply changing roles.

7-Eleven CEO Joe DePinto spent seven days in franchisees' and employees' shoes for the CBS show 'Undercover Boss.' Running himself ragged underscored for him that the way to lead is to support the troops.

"At the core, it's about support. I was an artillery guy. I was taught, 'There is this maneuver element out there — the infantry and the armory. Your job is to support them.' That's all we did. We worked to support those guys." - Joe DePinto, CEO 7-11

DePinto changed the mindset of the organization from one of top-down control to one of bottom up support. By "flipping the pyramid" he turned the organizational structure upside down. In the traditional model, the company was run by a "headquarters" but following DePinto's change, 7-11's old HQ was now a "support center."

What business programs like "Undercover Boss" regularly expose is how out-of-touch senior management is with the daily lives of not just their customers but their Frontline employees. A week, or even a day, at the Frontline leaves them with powerful insights and processes they are compelled to change.

7-11 is typical of any traditional business – built on a top-down pyramid of control. All the power is located at the top of the organization. When you put the Frontline at the top, people start to see what the goal of the organization is: not to support the management, but to support the people who interact with the customer. The pyramid structure exists because it served a purpose in the pre-digital age. How do you best allocate resources when resources are limited? Traditional structures are based on a limited supply – resources and information. Most organizations are organized silos of information. The reason the guy is the boss is because he has some information and knowledge that the others don't. When you work in an efficiency based organization, you work in a top-down power structure.

A lot of careers are built on keeping heads down and looking after the guy above you. That means being successful in this model is less about being creative and taking risk and more about delivering what your manager wants.

But in The Connection Economy, you don't have time to ask what your manager wants. You need to create your brand right here right now in the moments you touch customer lives. Pyramid structures become a *diseconomy*. There is no economic benefit to siloing information anymore. There is no benefit to scale. You don't need to invest in relationships with gatekeepers and silo owners.

When "support" (formerly "head office") gives the Frontline everything they need including the data, tools and permission to make a difference, the business moves at speed. A call center rep can issue a return straight away. A Genius employee can give you a new iPad from out of the back rather than return it to a warehouse for 2-4 weeks. Front desk staff can rip up a bill if you're unsatisfied. A marketing manager can make decisions based on what she sees right now in front of her. This is what the customer demands and anything less, in the Connection Economy, means you've lost her attention.

METRICS: LESS COMMISSION, MORE NPS

The most effective Frontlines don't reward their people with commissions (see Apple, LEGO and Zappos).

It seems logical to accept commissions as part of any Frontline structure because we've been doing it, unquestioned, for years. Yes, commissions drive short term sales but they don't foster long term relationships. Focus on long term metrics conducive to experience and loyalty.

One of the reasons we traditionally rely on commissions is that they are the only available data Frontline staff can work with. Individual sales figures have always been motivating because they give staff direct feedback on how they're doing. But, it's the feedback not the commission that's motivates employees. After all, everyone wants to feel they are making a difference.

Building motivation around commission has its problems. You attract a type of employee who thinks short term, often prioritizes their own interest above that of the team or company and views every contact as a sales opportunity. But, today we don't need to work purely on commissions. You can employ data like NPS to give employees a sense of ownership and significance.

Apple took a radical departure from traditional retailing by removing commissions from their Frontline staff. Apple employees were no longer measured on sales but on Net Promoter Score (NPS) or the level by which customers would recommend their experience to a friend. Every time you transact at an Apple Store you get a follow-up email or text that asks you to rate the experience, in particular how likely you would be to recommend it. That information is then relayed to store level and both managers and employees can get immediate feedback on how they're doing.

This doesn't just apply to retail or sales staff. Think how metrics like awareness and brand equity are used as a measure of success for marketing departments. They don't follow these metrics because they are the most effective, they follow them because they are often the only metrics available. When marketing teams aren't out there at the Frontline interacting with Fans and customers on a daily basis, how else are they going to know they make a difference apart from a number they're fed once every quarter?

Empowering your Frontline with metrics is key to staying agile in a fast moving environment.

Look at how Amazonian Fire Ants react to change quickly. If they sense heavy rain, they immediately start organizing themselves in small groups and forming life rafts capable of transporting complete colonies across the Amazon River. They don't wait for top-down commands to start their preparations.

Fire Ants are remarkably adaptable and robust as a species in an ever-changing environment. They are capable of building remarkable structures without any ability to sketch plans or visualize designs.

The key to their success is Frontline empowerment. Ants know how to act and react to change. They don't ask for permission. Today, there is no need to refer to someone else to get the latest sales and marketing data because it's right there in your hands on your smartphone. Employees and customers can access information straight away without routing through a headquarters, a VP of operations, a consultant or an agency.

"I worked for Apple Retail for a couple of years in college. During my time there they had implemented the net promoter system, and I truly loved it. Unfortunately I can't give an NPS opinion from a management perspective, but from an employee's perspective, it helped motivate me to do my best every day because anyone could be a detractor. It was also great when, during meetings, our management team compiled the NPS feedback and we got to hear verbatim what our customers thought of our service." - Cat Kobe (former Apple employee.)

Get your KPIs to the Frontline and close the feedback loop. Make the data as real time as possible. Empower staff to make decisions and read the data on their own decisions. Cut out the middleman. Increase the velocity of Frontline decision making and feedback.

Sharing the data with the Frontline staff is a big part of motivation and motivation creates a far more powerful positive brand experience than any ad campaign could ever do.

CAN APPLE STORE CONTINUE TO BUILD A BRAND WORTH TALKING ABOUT?

Retail is enjoying a renaissance and stores like Apple are at the forefront of the revival.

Competitors have taken a look at the success of Apple and are trying to replicate the formula. Samsung and Google have both tried their hand at experience stores with limited success. Often the problem is less about the efficacy of a store-based strategy and more about the baseline from which these brands operate. Apple built its store around empathy. Can Samsung and Google do the same? It's not a tap you can easily turn off and on, more a cultural trait that requires years of nurturing to become a marketing asset.

We already touched upon changes in the retail store in the earlier section on Apple. On that basis alone, it would suggest that while Apple will continue to grow as a brand that people talk about, it may decelerate long term as Apple "cashes in" on some of that goodwill.

It's also worth considering that Apple has new competition. Let's take a look at the popular Chinese brand Xiaomi:

- *Xiaomi is also opening 100 experience stores.*
- *Xiaomi recently sold out of the launch of its Mi Tablet in 2.7 seconds. You can now imagine what kind of scenes are going to unfold at their future experience stores.*
- *While Xiaomi attracts a lot of negative PR for its cheaper handsets, often citing "knockoffs" or technical problems with the codebase or stability, it's difficult to deny the Fans. Xiaomi does, indeed, have an inferior product in many customers' eyes and it has its issues, but are these criticisms any different than those leveled at Japanese*

auto manufacturers in the 1970s? Early pioneer exporters were berated for copying American models but it was their close contact with customers that helped their cars evolve at a faster pace. In time, not only were Japanese cars more reliable but they were soon becoming more popular. Honda and Toyota became the brands that people talked about, not in the pejorative but as the better brands.

- Multiplying a strong vocal Fan base with a retail Frontline creates a powerful proposition. We don't think Apple has faced such a similar threat. Other handset brands have tried to play the Apple game but none have brought both of these assets together to the table. It's quite possible Xiaomi will erode Apple's market, especially at the lower end, especially if Xiaomi can get students talking about the brand today.

Sure, it will take a long time and Apple will lean on government regulation to keep Xiaomi out through patent squabbles and media fear of anything Chinese, but in the end the truth will win out. Perhaps Xiaomi won't topple Apple but it will certainly provide a viable alternative in a market lacking real choice.

CHAPTER 11. STARBUCKS: BUILDING A BRAND ON EMPATHY, NOT EFFICIENCY

෯෯෯෯෯

CEO Starbucks - Howard Schultz

McDONALD's vs STARBUCKS:
EFFICIENCY vs EMPATHY

On January 31 1990, less than a year after the fall of the Berlin Wall, and in the spirit of Gorbachev's Perestroika, McDonald's arrived in Moscow's Pushkin Square.

Customers and onlookers alike turned up to gawp at the Golden Arches for up to 10 hours in the depth of Russia's harsh winter, holding menus handed out by staff that explained the ordering process. Some arrived from out of town with a weekend's reading, others just to use the hygienic washroom (a first in post-Communist Russia). 5 students flew 1,800 km from Armenia for the event. Many were among the 27,000 who had applied for a job at the new branch (only 630 were successful).

As Russia's burgeoning 200 million consumers awakened to the "delights" of the Capitalist West, McDonald's discovered that locally sourced potatoes didn't fit into the holes of their french fry processing machines. The answer to this predicament was typically McDonald's: source tried-and-tested potatoes from abroad. In a country famous for growing potatoes, McDonald's found it could shave cents off the cost of production by importing tanker-loads of frozen french fries cut from russet potatoes in the US.

It's this approach to solving the problem of business, namely a ruthless drive for efficiency, that makes McDonald's one of the most successful fast food franchises in the world. It's also this efficiency that makes the customer experience lousy. Although the ads tout the slogan "I'm lovin' it", nobody does.

They don't love the plastic chairs that lean forward rather than back to prevent customers getting comfortable. They don't love the staff whose meltdowns and spats regularly feature on YouTube. The word "McJob" has come to mean the lowest paid, most unfulfilling jobs our economy has to offer. Anti-obesity and anti-globalization campaigns aren't lovin' it too. Just like those all-important Millennial customers. In the US, Millennial spend on McDonald's grew only 0.3% in 2014, compared with 5.2% at rival Starbucks.

Ironically, Starbucks bears many similarities to McDonald's: a global brand and a menu of rather unhealthy, high-calorie, nutrient-free food. Yet, when it comes to how these brands are treated on social media, they live in parallel universes. McDonald's is the ultimate pariah. McDonald's is a media byword for obesity and fast food. Its CEO spends a large amount of his time lobbying to protect the brand from external pressure - media, educators and parents. By contrast, Starbucks consistently ranks in the top 10 of the most recommended and talked about brands.

Why?

The difference between McDonald's and Starbucks isn't one of product, but what lies at the heart of their brands. On the one hand, you have McDonald's, a brand built on Efficiency. On the other, Starbucks, built on Empathy.

Let's look at each to understand how these choices impact how customers experience the brand.

Ray Kroc, the man who turned McDonald's into the franchise empire we know today, once said that if you gave customers choice, there would be "chaos". He was instrumental in reducing the original McDonald's menu from over one hundred to just a handful of items. He also stopped the practice of roller-skating girls serving customers in the parking lots, forcing patrons to leave their own personal space and sit in the controlled confines of the restaurant.

Choice means inefficiency.

"The Customer is Always Right" is perhaps one of the most misleading business phrases of our time. What we take for granted as an empowering service mantra produces, like the potatoes, a standardized, efficient and flavorless experience. If the customer is always right, no matter what the customer says or does, the employee is always wrong. With this mantra, McDonald's is able to strip all Frontline staff of any decision-making capacity whatsoever. The default resolution for all interactions is the customer is always right, even when they're not.

The *Customer is Always Right* disempowers Frontline staff and removes the critical human touch from all interaction. It's efficient because it eliminates error, standardizing the process by turning people into robots. That's why the *Customer is Always Right*, is wrong.

Think of McDonald's as a machine or a factory. It strives to be the ultimate efficient model, reflected by the fact it's sold as a templated franchise all around the world. Don't mess around with the template, just do it. The training manual states burgers needed to be cooked for exactly 3 minutes on each side. Every aspect of the business was carefully planned to deliver a consistent experience. It's so efficient, that the whole business can be run by teenagers.

Everything about McDonald's is designed to be efficient: from the restaurant layout to the grilling techniques. And in this process there is nothing more inefficient than the human being. You see, people don't always follow the rules. People interpret process according to their own subjective evaluations. People make decisions.

Efficient models, like that of McDonald's, work by stripping all elements of humanity out of the model. McDonald's only hires humans because a) they are still cheaper than machines and b) we haven't developed machines intelligent enough yet to do their jobs. Come the day, they'll be the first inefficient link in the chain stripped out of the model. But, do we want food served by machines? Some will, but increasing numbers won't because we're not just buying the food. We're buying how these brands *make us feel*.

To make a process efficient, you must remove all risk and there is no bigger risk than the human being. A good example of this is the outsourced call center. The call center is outsourced to save money, not provide a better experience for the customer. Interactions are scripted. Operatives are even given false names, removing them of their natural identity. He's no longer Dilip but "Andy". They're not allowed to give you the name of their manager. Everything they do is "company policy." He hates it. We hate it. But, we continue to create this experience as long as we allow Efficiency to guide our business decisions.

Efficiency makes sense when you have limited resources. When you're running a factory, you don't want line workers messing around with the process, you want them to perform like robots with human intelligence. That is the most efficient, lowest risk and cheapest way of producing your widgets. You don't want *weird*, or *different* or *creative*. Just put the widget in the box.

When you're dealing with people, the factory model doesn't work anymore. Consider how the McDonald's model of business could apply to Zappos:

- Rigid, call center scripts
- Call Frontline employees "crew"
- Strict and punitive returns policies
- Standardized uniforms
- High churn recruitment environment
- Rigid, hierarchical structures

In the Connection Economy what counts is the inefficiency, the human touch. We want the stuff you can't scale.

In the 21st Century, you can only be so efficient. Efficiency for business is what management consultants would call "hygiene". It's like restaurant washrooms. You don't choose where to go based on the cleanliness of the W.C. but it will stop you going there again if it doesn't meet your standards.

By contrast, Empathy lies at the Heart of the Brand. Inefficiency is Empathy. Empathy makes us human: few animals have the ability to empathize with both other animals and their own species to the scale and depth humans are capable of. An absence of empathy is common in anti-social behavior. Criminals often lack the ability to empathize with the suffering of those they victimize.

Starbucks builds its brand on Empathy and it nurtures this through asking the right questions. McDonald's asks "how can we make a more efficient burger?" Starbucks, by contrast, asks "how can we make this the happiest experience of your day?"

Compare how these questions play out in how these brands are experienced by both customers and employees:

- Immovable seats vs comfortable leather chairs
- Homogenous eating space vs The 3rd Space
- The Customer is Always Right vs talking to regular customers
- Service staff vs Barista
- Faceless vs Howard Schultz
- McJob vs health insurance, benefits for employees

Today, people are willing to forego efficiency for the human touch. Customers shop around for locally sourced, organic food. They want to know the names of farmers who reared the livestock, are willing to line up for an hour on the sidewalk for a food truck to arrive and pay twice as much for a coffee if it means sitting in a comfortable leather arm chair, listening to piped jazz music.

Customers want inefficiencies. We want Baristas to call us by our name, we want to read chalk board daily menus written by the store manager, we want to know our staff live locally, idle awhile to talk to us and care about the things we care about. They feel our pain.

As journalist Chris Umiastowski from The Globe and Mail put it, "People enjoy coffee, and people enjoy hanging out with others while drinking coffee. I don't see this changing during my lifetime, no matter how much time we waste staring at screens." Brands are defined by this human touch and there is no bigger risk in business today than involving a human being.

Despite the recession, Starbucks continues to grow where McDonald's struggles. Take a look at their financials.

5 Year Stock Price Growth Comparison (2009-2014):

Starbucks:+361.9%
McDonald's: +69.94%

Starbucks has delivered a cumulative annual growth rate (CAGR) of 12% on revenue since 2011, while expanding its profit margin.

By contrast, the McDonald's machine struggles as explained in a Barron's article from Q4 2014:

"[McDonald's]... results have slowed, however. During the fourth quarter of last year, the company generated flat sales and earnings. Last month, same-store sales, a key measure of improvement at longstanding locations, fell for the fourth straight month. Management says it is working to improve value and streamline menus. Some analysts say McDonald's weathered a deep U.S. recession by heavily promoting its Dollar Menu, which brought in more lower-income customers, who are now struggling amid a widening U.S. wealth gap."

"McDonald's is trying to look and feel more like Starbucks," said Howard Penney, managing director at Hedgeye Risk Management LLC, who has covered the industry for 20 years, in a Bloomberg article. "It's actually hurting them, not helping them because the chain's competitive advantage is food not beverages and because making complicated coffee drinks slows down service."

"They basically now just hang a sign from the ceiling that says 'McCafe' over the espresso machine," Penney said. "It was rolled out very differently than it was first imagined."

Even though McDonald's can see how Starbucks is winning, it can't replicate it. You can't build Empathy into the heart of an Efficient brand. A machine will never *feel*. Empathy isn't something you sprinkle in a company's annual prospectus or something you can create by hiring an "Empathy manager," it's found at the heart of the Starbucks brand in the People, Culture and Metrics.

PEOPLE: UNDERSTAND THEIR PAIN

Empathy is ultimately about suffering. What is the pain that the customer feels on a daily basis?

We're not talking about physical pain but fear, emotion and other negative energies that cause internal suffering. If you can identify these pain points you can create exceptional brand experiences. But, identifying pain points starts with being Empathetic. You need to spend time with your Fans, your Ecosystem and work out what's not working. Feel into their problems. Don't ask for logical post-rationalizations. *Observe* behavior and emotions in situ.

Long ago, the son of a king of Persia was raised alongside the son of the king's senior advisor, who became his greatest friend.

When the prince ascended to the throne he asked his friend to write a history of men and the world so he could learn from it how best to act. His friend went away to consult historians and scholars, sages and wise men. Five years later he re-appeared in triumph with thirty-six volumes relating the entire history of the world, from creation to the young king's accession.

"Thirty-six volumes!" cried the king.

"How will I ever find the time to read them? I've so much to do running my kingdom. Please, my dear friend, condense your work for me."

The historian bowed, and went back to work on his history of men and the world. Two years later the king's friend sought out the king; he had a ten-volume version. The king was away at war with his enemies, and his friend eventually found him on a mountain top in the desert, directing the battle.

"This battle decides the fate of our kingdom. How can I find the time to read ten volumes? Please, old friend, abridge your history even more."

The king's friend bowed, went away and spent three years writing a single volume that accurately summarized his history of the world. When he returned to court, the king said:

"You're lucky, having the time to sit and think and write in peace and quiet. Whilst you've been doing that, I've been working on taxes and how to collect them. Reduce the pages of your history tenfold, and I'll spend an evening digesting them."

Two years later, the work was completed. But when his old friend the historian returned, the king was bedridden, and in terrible pain. His friend was himself now a white-haired, wrinkled elder.

"Well?" said the king with his dying breath. "The history of men - what is it?"

The historian gazed steadily at the king as he died, and said:

"They suffer, Your Majesty."

We all endure some degree of suffering in our daily life: smartphone screens crack, we are late for work stuck in traffic and we fall out with our loved ones.

As much as advertising seduces us with product benefits, what really motivates us is pain:

- Fear of missing out
- Fear of looking stupid
- Fear of isolation
- Fear of losing control

If you want proof, turn on the TV or read the newspaper. It's all about fear. You see, as much as we say happiness is an important part of our lives, it's not key to our survival as a species. Fear keeps us alive: fear of the night; fear of the saber-tooth tiger; fear of rival Stone Age tribes raiding our villages. We are far more motivated to avoid pain than to seek happiness, and it's this baseline of fear that creates the suffering we're talking about.

You could of course, just sell coffee. But then you're competing with cheaper rivals like McDonald's. Cheaper and faster. Starbucks, however, doesn't just sell coffee. Starbucks speaks to us emotionally. It understands our pain. Stick with this idea. It may sound far-fetched, but let's join a few dots here for the modern customer:

- *Howard Schultz, CEO, describes Starbucks as the "Third Place", the other 2 being home and work. The prime motivator to go to Starbucks isn't the product; that just gets Starbucks into the game. What keeps people there is the feeling they belong.*

- *The most profitable franchise in Starbucks is in Japan – ranked by Nationmaster as one of the unhappiest of all developed nations. The PiaPia restaurant in Tokyo recently posted a note in its window featuring a hand-drawn couple and a heart that have been crossed out with an explanation stating, "We will be refusing entry to all couples on December 24, with no exceptions!" Banning couples so not to make restaurant diners feel lonely. There you have it. Eating alone. The ultimate manifestation of a lonely culture.*

- *Goldman Sachs recently released a research report that includes a survey of 2,000 consumers' restaurant preferences. The results show that the under-34 demographic, which will soon be outspending baby boomers, is far more likely to buy anything from Starbucks than McDonald's – or any other food vendor.*

- Young people are also the loneliest generation. They grow up without the social space older generations once took for granted. 40 percent of adults in two recent surveys said they were lonely, up from 20 percent in the 1980s. A longitudinal study by American Psychological Association found that in 1991, 87% of parents said the family gets together every day around dinner or TV to catch up on each other's day. In 2001, that number went down to 81% and in 2011, it stood at 73%. 70% of UK residents say they wouldn't recognize all of their neighbors. In 1985, the average American had 3 close friends. By 2004, that number has dropped to 1. 25% of people surveyed said they have no one to confide in.

In short, the modern customer (especially the young one) is lonely and Starbucks is the solution to that pain.

Consider that Starbucks also hails from Seattle. Seattle was the #1 city for inbound migration in the US in the 90s. That meant more young Americans were moving to Seattle than any other city. That's a lot of young people, uprooted from their social networks, looking for a place to plug into.

It's not just Starbucks. Apple gets empathy too. The picture below shows a marketing document written by founding investor Mike Markkula in 1977 laying out on one page the 3 principles of Apple's marketing strategy.

The Apple Marketing Philosophy

Empathy
We will truly understand their needs better than any other company.

Focus
In order to do a good job of those things we decide to do we must eliminate all of the unimportant opportunities.

Impute
People DO judge a book by its cover.
We may have the best product, the highest quality, the most useful software etc.; if we present them in a slipshod manner, they will be perceived as slipshod; if we present them in a creative, professional manner, we will *impute* the desired qualities.

Mike Markkula
January 3, 1977

Notice the top item on the list? Empathy.

"We will truly understand their needs better than any other company."

Simple, direct, perfect. It's a promise Apple has kept until this day. Spending billions on traditional advertising doesn't necessarily build empathy. Spending billions on your Frontline, however, does. The Apple Genius crew training manual is stuffed with references to empathy and how to create environments and interactions conducive to understanding the customer. Apple understands, as it did 40 years ago, people don't buy stuff: they buy what stuff does for them. When you walk into the Apple store you're not buying an iPad or an iPhone but the whole experience, from the feeling of being special to the trust in the Genius store employee to look after you and give you what you want.

It's what makes Starbucks special too. If you were just selling coffee, you better know how to sell it faster and cheaper than McDonald's. Not many people can do that. But Starbucks isn't about being cheaper or faster, but rather understanding the customer better.

CULTURE: INCREASE TOUCH TIME

But how do you create empathy?

You don't need to. Employees already have the capacity to empathize. We're born with it. We are naturally empathetic. We possess the ability to share the emotions and feel the pain of others, regardless of culture or training. Organizations prevent us from empathizing. Organizations build walls between marketers and the customer.

Empathy is like the health of the organization. The more you unlock the natural flow of the organization (breaking down the walls), the more the health flows. Create a culture where employees know it's okay to empathize with employees.

If you want to increase Empathy, increase contact. Despite the power of social media, nothing can replace our analog nature. We are analog by design and analog contact happens offline. Real world contact reveals real world insights that help grow exceptional brands.

When you're stuck behind the wall of online market research or in-office focus groups, you might be sitting on top of reams of data, but it does little to create what you need - Empathy.

Consider, for example, the following case study from Cisco:

Cisco struggled for months with trying to improve its online process, but progress was slow. The breakthrough happened when Cisco sat the user in front of their customer experience team. It was the first time they had come face-to-face with a user in action and the first time they saw their frustrations and emotions in their real, offline, analog form.

Martin Hardee, Director for Cisco.com, cites the example of the password reset process. In 2011, it had a failure rate of 37%. After some initial work, they reduced the failure rate to 23% but there was still much to do to make the process user-friendly.

"These were sometimes complex systems, and implementing further improvements," Martin explains, "required coordinated effort from multiple IT teams, usability and experience design people, and even content editors."

But, when the tests were performed in situ, working alongside actual users (in the same room), they reduced the failure rate to 0%.

Bill Skeet, Senior Manager of Customer Experience for Cisco Digital Support states,

"Watching and hearing a real user struggle with the website creates a connection. People who were previously reserved and detached from the customer can become catalysts for change."

METRICS: BIG DATA ISN'T NECESSARILY THE ANSWER

Big Data is useful, but Big Data has its limits.

Big Data helps us add another dimension to the insights we have, but it should never become the insight. The problem with Big Data is that it's easy. It's also being pushed by every other consultant in the industry. That means it's easy to fall into the trap of just going with the flow.

We have to step back and look at the bigger picture here. Big Data may yield useful insights but it's never a benefit in isolation. The more we rely on the data, the less we become empathetic by nature. We stop going out there. We cut off the analog communication. We become more Efficient by default.

On the one hand, there's the accuracy of the data:

59% of 12-17 year olds admit lying about their age on social media profiles to create accounts. 16 year olds were the biggest offenders. 67% fudged their data.

On the other, more importantly, is the false sense of security that data gives us, in particular the action of collecting and receiving data:

In the 1970s, Gierek's Communist Polish Government spent 5 years soliciting all its agencies and data collectors on developing a long term production plan for the citizens. They had all the presentations, research and insight they thought they needed but when it came to effecting the plan they had omitted one small detail. Nowhere in the plan did the country have capacity to fabricate hairpins. Gierek's administration failed on one major detail because nowhere in this male dominated team of agency robotniks did anyone have the capacity to empathize with the needs of the country's womenfolk.

The rest, as they say, is history. The system didn't fail because of a lack of hairpins or, for that matter, a lack of data, but because of a lack of Empathy. Hairpins (or lack of them) are an embodiment of this shortcoming. The people and the politicians just didn't "get" each other.

It's easy to fall into a similar trap. Big Data may give us information, but it's information we hide behind, information that doesn't give us any real insight into the problem. Think of it as an illusion.

Researchers at the University of Pennsylvania found that by measuring language used in a user's status update they could predict, with 92% accuracy, the gender of the person. 92% is pretty accurate and it's tempting to start believing that data this accurate can solve our brand challenges.

But think again. If you were to look at the photo of the person posting the update, you could probably predict their gender with near 100% accuracy. By analyzing massive amounts of social media data, we can conclude that we are able to predict, with reasonable accuracy, what we already know. But, nothing can replace the power of actually going and seeing.

METRICS: MAKE FEEDBACK COUNT

Starbucks measures employees on customer feedback. A key part of this appraisal process is the "Customer Comment Card" which is a list of questions answered by Starbucks customers about their thoughts on both Starbucks employees and services.

Once a week, the leadership team reads through raw, unedited customer comment cards. "Sometimes it can be shocking to hear what they have to say, but it brings us directly to the level of the customer," said Margie Giuntini, VP of Retail Operations at Starbucks. "At the corporate level, it is easy to get disconnected from the customer."

Managers usually gives bonuses to employees that have scored well e.g. more than 70 out of 100 in the customer comment card. Managers and retail employees (baristas and cashiers) are also measuring each other's performances simply by observing how their workmates are doing.

If you want to create a more Empathetic culture, break down the walls. Create a direct connection between the feedback customers give and the rewards the company gives its employees. Until we make that connection, feedback is just noise, a distraction or a "nice to have". Making feedback count is the first step to empowering employees to create better brands.

CAN STARBUCKS CONTINUE TO BUILD A BRAND WORTH TALKING ABOUT?

There are 18 million photos tagged #starbucks on Instagram. Starbucks has more photos tagged than Coke, McDonald's and GoPro combined. That's no mean feat and certainly evidence that Starbucks is building a brand worth talking about.

On the upside, there are a number of positive signs:

- *Starbucks continues to grow through Earned Media. Starbucks spends less than 10% of what McDonald's spends on advertising. What Starbucks does spend tends to be search engine advertising (e.g. Google Adwords) aimed at specific promotions rather than any form of "Branding".*
- Starbucks continues to innovate in all directions - from mobile ordering to mobile payments. MyStarbucksIdea is a valuable asset in maintaining an ongoing dialog with Fans and understanding what's broken in the experience.

However, there are potential downsides worth noting:

- *Because Starbucks is one of the most talked about brands in the world, it's not afforded much breathing space. Howard Schultz's #racetogether strategy encouraging baristas to talk about race received a lot of public flack. As actor Rob Moore tweeted, "why doesn't Starbucks just focus on serving good coffee?" The fact that a Hollywood actor was willing to raise the question is also an encouraging sign; it's unlikely many would ask the question in defense of McDonald's.*
- *Record growth is already priced into Starbucks stock. That means anything but future record returns is going to undershoot expectations. Maintaining a focus on long*

term growth in the face of short term investor demands requires strong brand leadership. Starbucks has Schultz but as we've seen with Apple, shareholder politics and personal interests can derail a successful brand as soon as growth starts to slow.

- *And we can't consider Starbucks' fortunes without also looking at McDonald's. McDonalds is in retreat, soul-searching for a solution to its problems. That could go either way. McDonald's could bounce back as a Starbucks wannabe, offering a social space, a softer image and an empathetic approach to its customers. In that scenario, Starbucks would be competing with a bigger (albeit less authentic) rival. Conversely, McDonald's could bounce back as McDonald's in new clothes. (New menu, new brand, new colors, etc.) We think this is the more likely scenario given its history in such situations. In this situation, it will be other competitors in the fast casual dining market like Shake Shack and Chipotle who provide Starbucks with a bigger threat.*

- Starbucks has always struggled in certain markets like in Melbourne, Australia where the self-confessed coffee snobs were quick to pillory the brand for its low grade coffee. Starbucks retreated but it's important to understand that what the snobs don't get is that Starbucks doesn't sell coffee, rather social space. If Starbucks can re-enter these markets under the guise of a non-chain coffee store (which it is experiment) there is hope it can crack these last few tough nut markets that seem resistant to its presence.

CHAPTER 12. GOPRO: PUT THE CUSTOMER'S STORY AT THE HEART OF YOUR OWN BRAND NARRATIVE

დდდდდ

GoPro CEO - Nick Woodman

HOW JAMES KENNISON SAVED A DEER ONE THANKSGIVING

James Kenison's friend tagged him in a Facebook post one Thanksgiving.

In the post, a video of a deer stranded in the frozen Albert Lea Lake, in Freeborn County, southeast Minnesota was recorded by the local TV channel, KAAL TV. The deer had been there for 2 days now with online commenters offering up their solutions.

"Just shoot 'im!" said some.

"Please save him!" said others.

But how? The ice was too thin for emergency vehicles or snowmobiles. Local authorities decided not to respond.

Kenison, a police officer and dog handler, had an idea. He was also a weekend hovercrafting enthusiast who was used to skimming the lakes in propeller driven boats. Maybe they could somehow use one of their hovercrafts to get across the ice to the stranded animal.

The next day, Kenison and his father, Doug, set out on the hovercraft expecting the worst. The vehicle had never been tested on the ice; the stranded deer may already have been put down by the enthusiastic "Just shoot 'im!" lynch mob or the deer may itself have died of hypothermia on the lake, where temperatures can reach as low as -20C.

To their surprise they reached the deer and it was still alive, although barely conscious. Attaching a length of rope around its legs, they managed to haul it out of the icy river, saving not just the deer but two others from its herd in the process. It's a story that probably wouldn't have made it beyond a feature on the nightly local news except for the fact that Kenison captured the whole ordeal with a GoPro Hero 3 camera on his helmet.

Tina Marchman, a GoPro employee who regularly monitors video submissions on YouTube, reached out to Kenison and asked if they could use the footage in their marketing. In return for the latest GoPro equipment, Kenison agreed. Kenison's video amassed over 5,000,000 views and 27,000 likes on YouTube.

When asked about his newfound hero status, Kenison simply replied, "We just like hovering - so any chance to go out on them is an extra bonus." Kenison is not alone. There are 23,000 videos of hovercrafting shot with GoPro cameras on YouTube alone.

To achieve scale in such a defined niche is beyond the scope of any traditional marketing strategy. So how does GoPro do it? Not just hovercrafting but BMX, mountain biking, surf, skydiving, open water swimming, household pets, astronauts, car enthusiasts, musicians and yes, even midwives. GoPro does it with Brand Democracy: putting the customer's story at the heart of the brand.

NICK WOODMAN'S STORY

GoPro's CEO, Nick Woodman, fell in love with surfing at the age of 8. He saw tearouts from Surfer magazine plastered over a friend's house in Hawaii.

"I didn't even know that world existed," he recalls, "but from then on, I knew I wanted to live in it."

Woodman sold T-shirts in high school and attended UC San Diego for college, because it was close to the beach. He was initially rejected but he got the decision overturned. For the next 15 years his education was one of trying to find an excuse to go surf, live near the sea or hook up with other surf enthusiasts. He wanted to attend UC San Diego because it was close to the beach but got rejected and ended up inland at UC Berkeley. To his surprise he landed in a dorm with a whole host of other landlocked enthusiasts, joining a fraternity of surfers who kept him busy doing anything but studying.

"We got to wake up every morning and surf Black's," Woodman told his alma mater's paper. "Then we'd go to class, and then surf Black's, and then go to class."

He scraped by on his grades and eventually turned his attention to a web venture that coincided with his growing interest in technology. In 2000, he founded FunBug, an online games platform that rewarded players with prizes. Being in the right place (California) at the right time (Dot com boom) he managed to raise $4m for the venture, but coming up short on both revenues and second round funding meant Woodman's first foray into entrepreneurship ended as a disaster. The company folded, losing his investors all their money. His project achieved notoriety, being featured on the infamous (but now defunct) f*ckedcompany website alongside other notables such as PetsPark and Boo.

Deflecting some of the family pressure to get a "proper job" in finance, the ire of his investors and also in search of some time out, Woodman took off on a 5 month sabbatical surf adventure around Australia and the Indonesian islands.

It's here he hooked up with other surfers in search of the world's best waves.

"Every time one of us would get a sick barrel," recalls Woodman of his time in Indonesia, "we'd say to each other: 'Arghh! If only we had a camera!' Every surfer knows that feeling!"

At the time, high quality action sports equipment was expensive and difficult to transport in carry-on luggage. Standard DSLR cameras, too, had difficulty capturing the magic of being inside the barrel 100 feet away from the shore. So, Woodman began experimenting with attaching cameras to his board. He brought a contraption he'd made out of a broken surfboard leash and rubber bands that allowed him to dangle a Kodak disposable camera attached to his wrist.

He admits it wasn't user-friendly and the contraption would often break or whack the user in the face. It's then Woodman decided that he'd be better off attaching a camera to his wrist, so he went in search of straps. His first attempts captured grainy, shaky photos of the surf trip which he still keeps today. Surf friends were stoked at some of the footage. How could they get these straps too?

There was just one problem: The straps worked fine but the technology didn't. "Every camera I used would flood or break after a big wipeout," he says. "I realized I shouldn't be a strap company, but a camera company."

Returning from Indonesia, Woodman and his girlfriend set about raising money to create a prototype for the camera. But the timing wasn't right. He burned a few bridges at Funbug and didn't have the appetite to risk any more investor money.

So, rather than seek out VC finance, Woodman and his girlfriend spent three months traveling the coast, living out of his 1974 VW bus and selling bead-and-shell belts they had picked up for $1.90 apiece in Indonesia as $60 fashion accessories at concerts and flea markets. With the profits of their graft and a $35,000 family loan, Woodman continued refining his camera prototypes on his mother's sewing machine, moving back home to save money.

Then aged 27, he says he "checked out" from normal life, meaning divorcing himself from family and friends, locked away in his beachside bedroom for 18 to 20 hours a day, 7 days a week working on his plan.

"There were times when I felt like I was going crazy," Woodman says. "I had to walk to Starbucks to see people and not feel like I was just talking to myself all day. And then I'd walk back to my room and hole up. That's what it took for me."

Between sewing together old wetsuit material and drilling holes in raw plastic, Woodman was searching online and heading to trade shows for a camera he could modify and license as his own. After 2 years of research, Woodman found a cheap camera made in China by an unknown company called Hotax, originally marketed to snorkeling enthusiasts. He took a gamble mailing a $5,000 order to the company requesting specific designs for the camera and housing.

"I had no idea if I was dealing with a real factory or a sham," he says.

A few months later, his models came back, good enough as prototypes to provide props while hitting the trade show booths drumming up business. With a handful of early, working models in his pockets, Woodman and GoPro were in business. He sold his first GoPros in September 2004 at San Diego's Action Sports Retailer show and spent countless days ringing up surf shops around the country to convince them to put the original cameras on their shelves.

What happened next is pivotal in the GoPro story and key to the success of the brand. As he was beginning to demonstrate revenues and the feasibility of the business, Woodman made a conscious decision to bootstrap the business. Memories of FunBug haunted him and this time 'round he was determined to do it with minimum outside interference.

If he had started the business 4 years earlier, and rather than being a 2 man band hitting the action sports trade shows, selling his cameras out of the back of his VW, Woodman would have landed GoPro right in the middle of the dot com boom. He would be raising several million in early stage financing and the pressure would be on from day one to secure big name deals.

Investors would be squeezing Woodman to advertise. Their concern would be more driven by generating significant early sales and awareness of the brand so they could exit at a profit by selling on their first round stakes to second round investors. GoPro would be spending millions on X-Games sponsorships, Super Bowl ads, Paris Hilton and David Beckham. The investors would get their brand awareness. They'd get their profitable exit. Then Woodman and GoPro would be left struggling to compete with cheaper rivals attacking it from all sides.

Instead, bootstrapping the business from day one meant GoPro had no option but to leverage the product and customer content to do the marketing for them. This move may have appeared a compromise at the time but turns out to be the best decision they ever made.

In 2005, GoPro sold $350,000 worth of cameras mainly through Woodman's own personal hustle and relationships with surf and boutique sports stores, as well as 3 stints on QVC. "You wear it on your wrist like a watch," he told QVC viewers. "Flip it up to shoot."

By 2006, GoPro had eight employees, most of them doing sales. Half of the group worked out of a 1910 blacksmith's barn tucked behind the house Nick and Jill were renting in Pescadero, a coastal town of about 700 people nestled under the clouds between Half Moon Bay and Santa Cruz. The team put in 12- to 20-hour days in that redwood barn; five people and five cats.

"My nose would be dripping. Jill would wear a scarf. We were all freezing," recalls one of the early team members. "Nick sat up in a loft area, where he could hear all of our phone conversations and make sure we were making sales calls."

Sales were growing fast among action sports enthusiasts. GoPro staff noticed that customers were quick to share their videos online and in time people were calling the company asking for that camera they saw on YouTube.

"It took a few years to realize that there are a lot more people in the world that want to capture themselves doing what they want, what they love to do, their passions and interests, than there are that want to capture other people," said Woodman.

By 2009, GoPro generated $64 million in sales. It soon became the highest grossing digital imaging brand at Best Buy, knocking Sony off the number 1 spot with nearly $1 billion in sales. Today, it has 500 employees worldwide in 4 offices, 2 in China. When GoPro went public in 2014, Woodman retained 47% of the stock, making his holding worth over $5 billion.

"It was a classic 10-year overnight success case," Woodman said of his brand's rise to fame. Many didn't know where GoPro came from. All of a sudden it was everywhere without a single cent spent on traditional advertising.

The GoPro YouTube channel has over 240 million views. It's stuffed full of people just like Nick Woodman who wanted to tell their own story. There's Cory Kalanick and his heroic rescue of a kitten from a fire in Fresno; a 7 year old kid whose dad attached a GoPro to his BMX helmet; and James Cameron's deep sea dive into the Marianas Trench. Proud parents, adrenaline junkies and even a guy from New York's philharmonic orchestra who attached a GoPro to his trombone. One 90 second video shot of a mountain biker being hit by a gazelle in South Africa has over 15 million views.

Snowboarder Shaun White uses them on his runs in the Winter X games. The NFL tests them on their end zones to capture touchdowns. The Rolling Stones deployed them on stage and police forces have incorporated them in their training videos. When Woodman's own child was born, he wore a GoPro strapped to his chest in the delivery room.

Woodman didn't set out to redefine the market for digital imaging. He just wanted to shoot decent surfing photos. He wanted to give people the ultimate tool to help tell their own stories.

"Our goal," said Woodman, "was to create a celebration of inspired humans doing rad stuff around the world."

"This is Your Life: Be a Hero" - GoPro website.

PEOPLE: BRAND DEMOCRACY

In the Ogilvy era we, the marketers, told the brand story. We spent a lot of money doing just that. There was a lot of hoohah about the whole process with pitches and awards. Today, in the Connection Economy, we need to be taking a different role: from one of *storyteller* to one of story *facilitator*.

There are a million or more stories out there competing with ours for the attention of an audience. These stories are far more relevant. They come from real people who share those stories with their own networks. We can't compete anymore. Rather, we have to learn to play a role in helping customers tell their story instead.

Brand Democracy is a form of marketing where the customer tells the story, and every customer has a story to tell. Traditional top-down marketing has always been about telling the brand story. Whether on traditional or social media, the approach is always to use the medium to tell the official brand narrative. Brand Democracy, however, is about giving the customer the tools to tell their story.

As for using new media to create new ways to tell the brand story? That's new media but *business as usual.* Rather than see media as an opportunity to tell the brand story, look at it as a potential tool to help customers tell theirs.

Brand Democracy is the reason why companies like GoPro and Monster Energy can grow to multi-billion dollar valuations without advertising. It's also how they build sustainable Fan bases because their goal isn't the greater glory of their own brand, but giving their own people and customers a voice.

It's not who's telling your story but whose story you're telling that counts. In the modern brand narrative, the hero of the story is the customer. How can you use your marketing to make the customer the hero of the story? GoPro does this exceptionally well. The product is called "Hero". The website promises "be the hero".

The Ironman triathlon website, which GoPro is a partner in promoting, also delivers on that promise. The website welcomes the visitor into the grueling world of Ironman with the promise, "Become One."

Maybe not every customer is a downhill powder skier or endurance athlete but everyone wants to become the hero of their own story. It could be the trombonist who attaches the GoPro to his instrument, the father in the delivery room or the pet owner (yes pets can become heroes too). In every walk of life there is an opportunity. The start up business owner, the mentor to inner city kids, the artist, the teacher. Everyone has a story to tell and you can play a role in sharing those stories with others.

Don't run competitions or contests. Don't pick the heroes. Let Fans do that for themselves. Just provide the tools.

CULTURE: STAND BACK AND LET THE MAGIC HAPPEN

We must have faith in the customer's storytelling and step out of the loop. The more we try to hijack or interfere, the more we scare them away. Our role is to provide the platform, the space and the tools, not the conversation itself.

You can win by letting go.

We need to *curate* not *control*. The future marketing agency needs to be run by Curatives not Creatives.

We need to move from viewing customers as destinations for our marketing messages, to treating them as partners in its production.

When East Germany's communist leaders finally realized people were demonstrating openly on the streets in 1989, they offered concessions. They offered the people "elections". But the people refused because even though they could choose, they could only choose between official candidates.

We need to accept that customers can do this themselves and it's not going to blow up in our faces. Customers *can* do it. They'll do it when you're asleep. They'll do it on Christmas Day. They'll do it even when it costs them money. The point is that there is no more powerful or influential force in branding today than the amateur with a tool to share his or her story.

And that means accepting "cheap". Cheap means everybody and everything. Moving storytelling down the chain means it becomes more open, more democratic and cheaper. But cheaper doesn't mean worse, it actually means more relevant. A simple 140 character text message or photo can be more meaningful than a $5m advertising campaign if sent by the right person.

We aren't seeking production values or quality but shareability and relevance. Relevance is more important than quality and relevance often means the message is raw, unproduced and not what you'd traditionally allow in the brand template. But that doesn't matter.

We have to step down from the media ivory tower and look at the reality of what marketing messages are getting shared today.

47% of youth in the UK and USA shared selfies on Instagram.

When the Oxford Dictionary named "selfie" the "word of the year" the media world exploded with criticism:

- "A vain generation"
- "Narcissism
- "Fickle"
- "Self-obsessed"

Traditional media doesn't get it. Traditional media is the first to attack Selfies with all the above ammunition not because they lament the decline of societal standards but they fear the democratization of media. After all, what media rag isn't stuffed full of stories about vain, narcissistic, fickle, self-obsessed people like Kim Kardashian, or articles about getting that "beach body"?

When Van Gogh paints a self-portrait, it's art. Nobody's howling protests about vanity or narcissism now. It's a $25m masterpiece. Be aware of how traditional media plays power games. Traditional doesn't like it. It fears cheap. But you don't have to. Cheap is the future because cheap means *everybody*.

We've been here before. Radical technologies that allow everyone to tell their story always come under attack from those that stand to lose out. We saw it before with the printing press. Think of modern technology as a printing press too. Doesn't seem so radical. Print is an old technology, so how is it relevant here? Let's take a step back and look at how the printing press changed things back then.

The original printing press revolutionized storytelling and freed it from a controlling elite and democratized it for the masses.

Before the printing press, books were scarce. Books were handwritten works of art that took teams of monks (in large halls called scriptoriums) years to produce, in gold ink and on vellum. Because books were so valuable, storytelling remained the preserve of a rich media elite: the clergy and landed gentry. Books were written in Latin, a language few except the elite understood and often locked away or if on public display, chained to a pulpit.

The printing press disrupted storytelling. After its arrival, normal folk began printing their own stories. These weren't stories about the nobility and their religious piety but everyday people and their lives: from the seditious "Robin Hood", to the exotic "Arabian Nights", to the whimsical "Tales of the Savage Girl of the Forests of Champagne."

Because ordinary people could tell ordinary stories, the power structure of society changed. First there was the printing of the Bible in non-Latin languages like German, Dutch and English. Then there was the growth of social spaces like coffeehouses fueled by this rapid exchange of communication. Newspapers, pamphlets and circulars began to appear carrying with them new ideas like equality and democracy. It's of no coincidence that Benjamin Franklin was a book seller by trade and spent much of his formative years in the coffeehouses of London and Paris absorbing the new zeitgeist brought about by the printing press.

We are seeing a similar shift. The important point to remember is that organizations that stand in the way or interfere will lose out. All brands must decide on which side of the fence they sit - are they protecting high value official content or helping customers tell their unofficial, everyday stories?

Look at how traditional media reacts when ordinary people find their voice. In September 2011, the BBC ran an article titled "the ordinary people who stole the show" referring to a group of "ordinary" bloggers who upstaged the qualified fashionistas from the print and broadcast world to provide the best insight into London's fashion week. Alex Murray comments "... bloggers have been chipping away at the mainstream media as more and more people want to hear about fashion from people who apply it to everyday life."

This "chipping away" is part the investment these amateurs have in the show (they do it for love) and part the risks they can take because they are freed from the organizational yoke. Fashion blogs come in all shapes and sizes - from fashion obsessed teens like Tavi Gevinson (15) who started her blog Style Rookie at 11 to the more sartorial Bryanboy. Each has their own dedicated following, each a line of influence. But, the industry has refused to concede that, while important, these amateurs are the future.

"Newspaper fashion editors have got enormous experience and know what they're talking about," said Lisa Armstrong of the Daily Telegraph (...So teens don't know what they're talking about, right?)

Today in the Connection Economy, everybody has their own printing press. Every mobile phone, YouTube account, laptop PC and Tweet is a printing press. You don't need to be qualified. You don't need to be an experienced newspaper editor or journalist. You don't need to be rich, pious or landed to do it, *you just need an idea.* You don't need to wait to be picked or for permission; telling your story in your own hands.

As with the first printing press, observers weren't fully cognizant of the impact of this technology on society. At the time, we just thought it a series of random events, but the printing press brought about The Reformation, the Enlightenment, The Age of Reason, modern scientific thought and, ultimately, democracy. Today, too, we are just actors within a series of events. Indeed, the term "Reformation" wasn't invented until 200 years after the fact. Similarly, we exist in a time of great change but it's only with hindsight that we will understand what's going on today.

The Big Idea doesn't want to go lightly. It wants to stay. It wants to adapt, and stay on the agenda. Too much money, too many relationships, too many egos are tied up with the Big Idea.

"It speaks to the culture of the nation—it's saying, 'We're listening to you, America, and giving you the stuff that you want.'" Kate Sirkin, the global research director of Starcom MediaVest Group, an ad agency in New York, on the company's plans to let Super Bowl viewers *control the ads.*

Ad agencies don't get it. People don't want to control ads, they want control.

METRICS: ACCEPT THAT BRAND DEMOCRACY TAKES TIME

The shift to Brand Democracy will take time. People are so used to other people telling the story for them that it will take a long time before we finally get used to doing it ourselves.

Take a look at the youth market. This generation grows up thinking, "well of course." Uploading videos to YouTube, sharing on Instagram or self-publishing, they are leading the way. Youth lead the charge in change, telling and sharing their own everyday stories. Older generations are still waiting for others to do it for them.

For more than 50 years we've become accustomed to media telling the story for us. When media steps back and gives us a platform to tell our own story we are naturally suspicious, we wonder what to do, we look to others for answers. That's why Brand Democracy isn't going to happen overnight.

CAN GOPRO CONTINUE TO BUILD A BRAND WORTH TALKING ABOUT?

GoPro's tenure as one of the world's most talked about brands seems a very difficult one to maintain long term.

GoPro will struggle long term to compete with new entrants:

- *On the one side you have upstarts like Xiaomi offering GoPro clones for 1/5 of the price. The sheer disparity in pricing will raise doubts even in the minds of GoPro's most ardent Fans.*
- On the other side, there is the constant looming threat of an Apple moving into this space. Apple can move in mysterious ways. Watch, TV and auto manufacturers were all blindsided by Apple's market entry.

Perhaps GoPro will be acquired or tie up with a larger brand to buy into much-needed distribution partnerships. At present, GoPro demand outstrips supply. Every time a customer reaches a "sold out" page, they turn to alternatives. There aren't many credible players to fill the gap but, as stated above, there soon could be. Samsung or Microsoft could do well to acquire GoPro and create a powerful Fan base for their wider product base. But, acquisition raises its own issues. Cisco acquired Pure Digital's Flip and mothballed a project that was GoPro before its time.

GoPro is currently moving into the content space. Perhaps, like Amazon, GoPro sees its long term revenues coming from the ability to serve content on its device. If this is the case it will need massive scale and resources to remain the most talked about brand. Red Bull is already in that space with the creation of its Media House. Will GoPro compete or partner?

GoPro's advantage is built on being first to market combined with a very vocal Fan base. But, being new raises its own challenges. GoPro could see its market attacked from either side; it could lose focus by diverting resources into content production rather than creation. Either way, it has a 12-18 month window where it will continue to rise and continue to dominate conversations.

CHAPTER 13. SUMMARY

క్తిక్తిక్తిక్తిక్తి

In this book, we started out looking at how the rules have changed. Brands that were once successful (e.g. Nokia) are now struggling to play by the new rules.

We set this out in the context of the Tin Man's quest in the Wizard of Oz. Everybody involved in marketing today has to resist the temptation to seek all the answers in The Emerald City. Your brand's heart, the truth about what people feel when they experience your brand, the daily mechanics that create that experience don't lie with some expert, external agency but within your own company: your People, Culture and Metrics.

But, despite this knowledge, brands still struggle because they are a victim of their own success. Change is hard. They became successful on the back of a marketing model that was highly effective in the 20th century. Not long into the 21st, the wheels of their marketing success fell off. We are creatures of habit. Many would rather continue doing the ineffective but *familiar* than the effective and *unfamiliar*.

This is the shift between the Ogilvy Era and the Connection Economy. The methods of the Ogilvy Era - defining brand outside the company - no longer work like they used to. That's why it takes brands like Zappos to show us how marketing works in the Connection Economy.

Rather than being a mystical, intangible concept as it once was in the Ogilvy Era, we can deconstruct the brand experience today into its core components: People, Culture and Metrics. This is what we call "The Heart of the Brand." The "Heart" is an important metaphor because it belongs inside the company.

Heart is also emotion. While we readily use terms like "Like", "Friend" and "Fan" in the context of marketing today, we have to realize their true meanings have been co-opted by social media. What counts isn't a million Facebook Likes but how much your customers Love your product. You can't measure Love with traditional metrics as they're all skewed towards being Liked. You have to use new metrics, like Earned Media recommendation, Net Promoter Score or word of mouth.

Behind every great brand in the Connection Economy are great people. In the LEGO case study, we looked at how one of the most successful brand turnaround stories of the modern era was built on people, in particular Fans. LEGO took its Fans and placed them in the middle of the business. The LEGO brand starts and ends with its Fans. Not only does this make their marketing far more effective, the business has become more productive, less wasteful and more profitable.

Great brands in the Connection Economy are able to show us that you can do this without advertising. Perhaps no more is this true that the sector that traditionally needs advertising the most: soda. Traditional soda marketing embodies the spirit of The Ogilvy Era - Big Ideas, big campaigns and big celebrity endorsements. But, Monster Energy Drinks has proven that you can do it differently. By focusing on word of mouth, Earned Media and building a brand through its own people, Monster has grown to become (at times) more profitable per employee than Apple.

"Cool" new marketing ideas may be possible if you're a "cool" brand by nature, such as an energy drink, but what if you're not? What if you're operating in a less exciting, more restrictive sector like an airline? Southwest Airline demonstrates it's possible to build a brand from the inside in this sector too. You don't need expensive campaigns or fleet redesigns to make an impact. In fact, these traditional marketing techniques often fall apart when customers actually experience your brand through interaction with your staff on a daily basis. We can no longer manager and control brands like we used to. Brands happen. The only way we can make those brands happen in favorable ways is to do our best to empower our own people to nurture the best experiences.

Building a brand with heart is within every marketer's grasp. Even a small Taco joint like Wahoo's has been able to do it. The key isn't to seek out celebrities and agencies who can grow your brand, but to find an Ecosystem where you belong. You could be a bank connecting with local startups or an insurance company with travel bloggers. Wherever your people already have networks is where you need to start building your brand. Wahoo's did this with surf. It's this symbiosis, bringing the Ecosystem into the heart of the brand, that helped Wahoo's grow from a single Taco joint in Costa Mesa to the $100m enterprise it is today.

Marketers easily get distracted. As we already discussed, brand can appear mysterious and complex if you let the mysticism of the Ogilvy Era get in the way. Apple's a good case in point. People talk of design philosophy or Steve Jobs' genius. But, the reality is that you can see and replicate the mechanics of Apple's marketing success in how it built its marketing at the Frontline with empathy at the heart of their strategy. In Apple's case, the Frontline is its retail store but this isn't the only kind of Frontline: events, communities and call centers are all examples of where the marketing rubber hits the road, where customers experience your brand. It's here in the Connection Economy that your brand lives and dies.

In the Starbucks vs McDonald's case study we looked at two fundamentally similar restaurants who produced vastly different results. McDonald's is struggling, especially with younger customers. By contrast, Starbucks is flourishing. And it's not about price, either. Starbucks charges 40% more than its nearest chain rival for coffee. The answer lies in Empathy. Starbucks built its brand on Empathy and that starts inside the Heart of the Brand. By contrast, McDonald's is built on Efficiency, like a machine. But customers have all the Efficiency they need these days. They'll pay more for inefficiencies, if they think that will solve the problems they face on a daily basis, like loneliness. These are the things you can't put a price on.

And finally, we ended with GoPro. GoPro's decision not to build a business through heavy external investment and advertising was its smartest move. This billion dollar brand was forced to turn to customers to do the marketing for it. Rather than becoming a compromise, it was a strategy that made the brand. GoPro's brand isn't defined by external agencies but by how customers use the cameras to tell their stories on a daily basis. And it's this Brand Democracy that is also redefining other industries too. In the Connection Economy, customers look at your marketing and ask, "where am I in this story?" Simply adopting social media is not enough. What defines brands today isn't choices in media but choices in mindset. How can you put the customer at the heart of your brand? How can you make the customer the hero of your story?

Not all these stories will work for your company, but some will. Start today. Like the Tin Man you risk an expensive and exhausting quest to find your brand's heart if you seek it outside of your company. Those days are over. Today, we have plenty of robust case studies like those in this book that should give you the green light to make change inside your company. They can do it. So can you.

CHAPTER 14. NEXT STEPS

✤✤✤✤✤

3 STEPS TO PUT BRAND LOVE ON THE AGENDA

We wrote this book because we believe there is a better way to build brands worth talking about.

The challenge now for you is to make that change within your own business and move your model of marketing from the Ogilvy Era to the Connection Economy.

You're probably asking, "where do I start?"

A) START WITH METRICS

From our experience, the first battle is to win on the Metrics. Metrics are pivot points of change. Because all organizations pivot on the way they measure and reward their people, small changes in Metrics can yield large results in behavior.

Make a commitment to stop going after quantity and awareness, and start going after quality and attention.

By making that commitment you will also attract the right people to you. Surround yourself with these people. You only need a small flame to build a fire. Small flames are how to approach this challenge. Don't change the metrics; focus on the right ones. Changing the metrics is disruptive.

Rather than being disruptive and tasking your whole organization to go into the forest and gather wood, keep it low key, keep it focused on a small group of change-makers who "get it". Any sized flame will eventually bring water to a boil.

What we're trying to prove here isn't that you can set the world alight, but that you can boil the water.

B) EVOLVE THE CULTURE

Rather than make this a battle about one metric vs another, focus on evolution. Maintain the status quo, but give the newcomers space too. Don't jettison the existing marketing strategies without a 2nd act to turn to.

Once you can demonstrate the concept, you need a Culture that can maintain the momentum of your small fire long term.

Use the metrics to evolve your Culture and practices. Add your requirements to the top of future agency briefs. Create a space for people to talk about long term relationships and Fans. Give your people time to get "out there" and talk to the Fans, feel the market and learn about brands that are doing it right (even if they're in different industries).

C) ATTRACT THE RIGHT PEOPLE

By evolving the Culture and tailoring the briefs with your new focus on Metrics, you will find the right people magnetized and the wrong people repelled from your brand. Your People should become self-selecting. Over time this will play out in recruitment policy and internal selection but in the short term it's reflected in choosing the right agency and the People naturally attracted to your project.

A key part of People, Culture and Metrics is access to case studies and opinions that you can both learn from and bounce ideas with. That's why we want to help you continue this journey.

2 WAYS TO KEEP THE BRAND LOVE MOMENTUM GOING

Here's two ways you can get started:

1) Shoot an email to theguys@brandlovebook.com

That email will land in the inbox of Graham, Jamal and Paul. You can send us a "hello", feedback or hate mail. We also want to hear from you if:
* You want to discuss how we can help make these ideas work for your brand
* You need a speaker for your conference or comment for your publication

2) Get the BONUS PRESENTATION

You got this far. We'd like to reward your perseverance! We put together a short presentation available exclusively to readers. This presentation is a great way for you to visualize some of the ideas in this book and share them with your colleagues. You can download it here by joining our list. Enter your email and get the download free. Once you're in, you'll also get access to regular updates on reader bonuses such as audio interviews with industry marketing experts and CMOs on the stories in this book:

Click here to download the bonus presentation FREE:
http://www.BrandLoveBook.com/readerbonus

HELP US IMPROVE THIS BOOK
& SHARE THE MESSAGE

All business books rely on feedback. Whether good or bad, we want to hear what you think. Did this book help you? Is there something missing? Would you like to see more information on one of the stories? Are you feeling inspired?

Whatever you have to say, share it. Every review gets published, and we will read every one.

You can help us improve Brand Love: How to Build a Brand Worth Talking About and help potential readers discover it too by leaving a short review on Amazon:

http://www.amazon.com/dp/B00VBPBU1G
http://www.amazon.co.uk/dp/B00VBPBU1G
http://www.amazon.de/dp/B00VBPBU1G

Not your store? Just change the end URL to your local store.

Thank you,

Graham Brown
Jamal Benmiloud
Paul O'Shannessey